THE TEA LOVER'S BIBLE

The Complete Guide to Exploring the World of Tea and Its Health Benefits - Learn About Traditions, Qualities, and Recipes

Lydia Merrill

BONUS LIBER

Published by Bonus Liber (www.bonusliber.com)
Edited by Melissa Fields
Book Cover by Grant Coleman

"No matter where you are in the world, you are at home when tea is served."

– Earlene Grey

Contents

Introduction

Tea is a magical drink. It's so much more than a simple cup of hot water and plant leaves. It's a gateway to a world of flavors, aromas, warmth, and community.

But the tea world can be intimidating for newcomers—especially if you're new to the idea of drinking tea as an experience rather than just something to drink. There are so many different types of tea, from black tea to white tea to oolong and pu'erh. Each type has its own set of rules and its own way of being prepared and consumed. And it goes on and on from there!

The Tea Lover's Bible is here to make sure that you don't get lost in the labyrinthine world of tea knowledge. This guide will take you step-by-step through every aspect of how to enjoy the best teas available—from how they're harvested and processed to how they taste and smell when brewed correctly (and what happens when they aren't). We'll cover everything from the hidden health benefits of herbal teas to pairing foods with teas—and even some ideas for serving them up in style!

Tea is more than just a drink. For many people, it is a ritual and a way of life. The preparation and enjoyment of tea can be a meditative and calming experience. The act of drinking tea can be seen as a way to connect with others and with the present moment. The philosophy of tea often focuses on mindfulness, simplicity, and harmony. It can be seen as a way to find balance and inner peace in a hectic world.

In this book, I will also delve into the rituals and customs associated with tea drinking and provide tips for brewing the perfect cup. You will discover how to cook using tea as an ingredient or how to make fantastic tea-infused cocktails for your parties.

Whether you are a seasoned tea connoisseur or just starting to discover the world of tea, this guide will provide a wealth of knowledge and inspiration. You will learn how to create your own tea garden from scratch and produce the leaves you need for your creative tea recipes.

So sit back, relax, and let's take a journey into the world of tea!

CHAPTER ONE
Tea Fundamentals

History

Tea has a rich and storied history dating back to ancient China. According to legend, tea was discovered by the Chinese Emperor Shennong in 2737 BC when some leaves from a nearby tree fell into his boiling water. The Emperor found the resulting drink refreshing and invigorating, and thus the tradition of tea drinking was born.

For centuries, tea was enjoyed exclusively by the elite in China, as it was considered a luxury item. It was often used as a currency and gifted to dignitaries and rulers as a sign of respect and friendship.

In the 8th century, tea was introduced to Japan by Buddhist monks who had traveled to China to study. The Japanese quickly embraced the drink, which became an integral part of their culture, with tea ceremonies held to honor guests and celebrate important events.

During the Ming Dynasty (1368-1644), tea drinking became more widespread in China as the cultivation of tea plants became more efficient and tea production increased. Tea houses sprang up all over the country, offering a place for people to gather and enjoy the drink.

In the 17th century, tea was introduced to Europe by Dutch traders who had been trading with the Chinese. The drink quickly became popular among the elite and was often served at lavish tea parties. In the 18th century, tea became even more popular in England by establishing tea gardens and opening many tea shops.

In the 19th century, the British began colonizing India and soon discovered the region was ideal for growing tea. British tea companies began planting tea gardens and importing workers from China and other parts of Asia to work on the plantations. This led to the creation of the British East India Company, which became one of the largest tea producers in the world.

Today, tea is loved by people of all ages and backgrounds and has become one of the most popular beverages in the world. It is grown in many countries, including China, India, Japan, and Sri Lanka, and comes in wide varieties, including black, green, oolong, and white.

Curious Facts

Tea has a rich history that is filled with interesting facts and stories. Here are just a few of the most curious anecdotes about tea:

Tea in the American Revolution

In 1773, British colonists in Boston were outraged by a tax on tea imposed by the British government. In protest, they boarded British ships in the harbor and threw the tea overboard in an event known as the Boston Tea Party. This act of rebellion was a significant event that helped to spark the American Revolution.

Tea was once used as currency

In the early days of the tea trade, the leaves were so valuable that they were used as a form of currency in some parts of the world. In Tibet, for example, tea bricks were used as money and were even accepted as legal tender by the government.

Tea is the second most consumed beverage in the world

After water, tea is the most popular beverage in the world. People of all ages and cultures enjoy it, and it is estimated that over 3 million tons of tea are consumed each year.

Tea bags were developed in the United States by accident

In 1908, a New York tea importer named Thomas Sullivan sent samples of his tea to potential customers in small silk bags. Some customers mistakenly believed that the tea was meant to be brewed inside the bag, and the idea of the tea bag was born.

Americans tasted their first iced tea at the World's Fair in St. Louis, Missouri (1904)

At the time, iced tea was a new and exotic drink that originated in the southern United States. It quickly gained popularity among fairgoers and soon became a staple at summer gatherings and picnics across the country. Today, iced tea is a beloved American beverage enjoyed by millions of people.

Tea causes less 'caffeine crash' than coffee

This is because tea contains less caffeine than coffee, and the caffeine in tea is released more slowly into the bloodstream. Additionally, tea contains other compounds that can help reduce caffeine's effects and prevent a crash. For example, theanine, a natural amino acid found in tea, has been shown to promote relaxation and reduce anxiety.

Tea Cultivation Explored

Tea is derived from the leaves of the Camellia sinensis plant, which is native to Asia. Tea has been cultivated for thousands of years, and many different methods are used to grow and harvest this versatile plant.

Tea is typically grown at high elevations in areas with cool temperatures and plenty of rainfall. The soil must be well-drained and rich in nutrients, as tea plants require plenty of water and nutrients to thrive.

Once a suitable location has been chosen, the tea plants must be carefully nurtured and tended. Tea plants are typically grown from cuttings or young plants, which are carefully transplanted into the ground. The plants are spaced out to allow plenty of room to grow and carefully watered and fertilized to promote healthy growth.

As the tea plants grow, they must be pruned and trained to encourage the growth of healthy leaves and stems. The plants are typically grown in rows, with each plant carefully trained to grow in a specific direction. This allows the leaves to be easily harvested and ensures that the plants are not damaged during the harvesting process.

When the tea plants are mature, they are ready to be harvested. The leaves are carefully plucked by hand, selecting only the most tender and flavorful leaves. These leaves are then carefully processed to preserve their flavor and aroma.

The first step in processing the tea leaves is withering them, which removes excess moisture and makes them more pliable. The leaves are then rolled or crushed, which helps to release the tea's natural oils and flavors. Finally, the leaves are dried and sorted to create different types of tea.

There are many different types of tea, and each type is created using different cultivation and processing methods. Green tea, for example, is made from leaves that are quickly steamed or heated to stop the oxidation process. On the other hand, black tea is made from leaves that are allowed to fully oxidize, giving the tea its deep, rich flavor.

Tea Plants

Tea plants are perennial plants, meaning they have a lifespan of more than two years and will continue to grow and produce leaves and flowers each year. This is an important characteristic of tea plants, as it allows for a consistent and sustained harvest of tea leaves for tea production.

Tea plants are typically grown in tea gardens or plantations, where they are carefully cultivated and nurtured to produce high-quality tea leaves. Tea plants can reach heights of up to 15 feet and have glossy, dark green leaves and small, white or pink flowers. Tea plants can take several years to mature and produce leaves suitable for tea production, with the first harvest typically occurring after three to four years.

Tea is a valuable source of income for many farmers and communities in tea-growing regions. Tea production is a labor-intensive process that involves several steps, including plucking, withering, rolling, oxidizing, and drying the tea leaves. The tea leaves are then sorted and graded according to their quality, size, and flavor and then packaged for sale and distribution.

Tea plants can continue to grow and produce leaves for many years, with some plants living for up to 100 years. However, tea plants can be affected by various diseases and pests, such as the tea mosaic virus and tea red spider mite, damaging the plants and reducing their productivity. Therefore, tea farmers must take measures to protect and maintain the health of their tea plants, such as using organic pesticides and fertilizers, pruning the plants, and providing the plants with adequate water and nutrients.

Tea Growing Regions

Tea is a popular beverage enjoyed worldwide, with various regions known for their unique tea cultivation methods and flavors. While many people may be familiar with the Chinese and Indian origins of tea, several different geographical areas contribute to the global tea industry.

One of the most well-known regions for tea cultivation is China, which has been producing tea for over 5,000 years. The country is known for its diverse range of teas, including green, black, oolong, and white. The famous Chinese tea-growing regions of Yunnan, Fujian, and Zhejiang are known for their high-quality teas, with different terroirs and climates contributing to the unique flavors of each area.

Another major tea-producing region is India, which is the largest producer and consumer of tea in the world. The country is known for its black teas, which are often blended with other flavors to create popular blends like chai tea. The northeastern states of Assam and Darjeeling are particularly well-known for their tea production, with their unique climatic and soil conditions providing the perfect environment for growing tea.

Sri Lanka, formerly known as Ceylon, is another important tea-producing region. The country is renowned for its high-quality black teas, known for their bright and full-bodied flavors. The country's central highlands are home to some of the world's best tea estates, with the Kandy, Nuwara Eliya, and Uva regions known for their exceptional teas.

Japan is also known for its high-quality green teas, which are carefully crafted using traditional methods. The Shizuoka and Kagoshima regions are particularly well-known for their tea production, with the latter being known for its award-winning sencha and gyokuro teas.

In addition to these regions, other countries such as Kenya, Vietnam, and Indonesia also contribute to the global tea industry. Each region has its own unique climatic and soil conditions, which contribute to the flavor and quality of the tea produced.

From Leaf to Cup: A Guide to Tea Production

Tea production involves several steps, starting with processing tea leaves and ending with packaging the finished product. While the specific methods and techniques used can vary depending on the type of tea being produced, most teas go through a similar series of stages.

The first step in tea production is the plucking of the tea leaves. This is typically done by hand and involves selecting the youngest and most tender leaves from the tea plant. The leaves are carefully plucked to ensure they are not damaged, as this can affect the flavor and quality of the tea.

After the leaves have been plucked, they are transported to a tea factory for processing. Here, the leaves undergo several steps to remove moisture and preserve their flavor. One common method for doing this is withering, in which the leaves are spread out on large trays and wilt for several hours. This reduces the moisture content of the leaves and makes them more pliable for the next step in the process.

The next step in tea production is rolling, which involves pressing and shaping the leaves to release their flavor. The leaves are rolled by hand or machine, and this process can either be done gently or more aggressively, depending on the type of tea being produced. For example, green teas are typically rolled more gently to preserve their delicate flavor, while black teas are rolled more aggressively to release their bold, robust flavor.

After rolling, the leaves are left to oxidize or "ferment" in a controlled environment. This process, also known as fermentation, helps to develop the tea's characteristic color, flavor, and aroma. Then, the leaves are dried to remove any remaining moisture. This is typically done using hot air, but some teas are dried using a method called pan firing, in which the leaves are placed in a hot pan and stirred until they are dry. This process helps to preserve the flavor and aroma of the tea leaves.

Once the leaves are dry, they are sorted and graded according to their size and quality. The leaves are then packaged and shipped to tea companies, where they are blended with other teas to create the various flavors and varieties of tea available on the market.

About Fermentation

Tea oxidation, also known as tea fermentation, is a crucial step in the production of many types of tea. It involves exposing the tea leaves to oxygen, which causes chemical reactions that alter the tea's color, flavor, and aroma.

There are two main types of tea oxidation: natural oxidation and controlled oxidation. Natural oxidation occurs when the tea leaves are left in a warm and humid environment, allowing the enzymes present in the leaves to react with the oxygen in the air. This process can take several days or weeks, depending on the type of tea being produced.

Controlled oxidation, on the other hand, is a more precise and rapid process typically used in producing black and oolong teas. In this process, the tea leaves are carefully exposed to a controlled amount of oxygen, which is typically achieved through mechanical means such as tumbling or rolling the leaves. This process typically takes only a few hours and allows for a more consistent and predictable outcome.

Both natural and controlled oxidation plays an essential role in the final flavor and aroma of the tea. In natural oxidation, the enzymes in the tea leaves break down the complex molecules in the leaves, releasing various volatile compounds that give the tea its characteristic flavor and aroma. In controlled oxidation, the exposure to oxygen allows for the development of complex and nuanced flavors, with different types of tea requiring different levels of oxidation to achieve their desired characteristics.

The oxidation process also affects the color of the tea. The leaves retain their green color in the case of green tea, which is not oxidized. In black tea, which is fully oxidized, the leaves turn a dark brown or black color. Oolong tea, which is partially oxidized, falls somewhere in between, with the leaves turning a reddish-brown color.

The oxidation process is not only important for the flavor and aroma of the tea, but it also has an impact on its health benefits. For example, black tea, which is fully oxidized, contains higher levels of theaflavins and thearubigins, which are powerful antioxidants that can help protect against heart disease and cancer. On the other hand, green tea, which is not oxidized, contains higher levels of catechins, which are also powerful antioxidants with numerous health benefits.

Sustainability

Sustainability is a concept that has gained significant traction in recent years, particularly in the food and beverage industry. The idea is simple: to ensure that the resources we use today do not compromise the ability of future generations to meet their own needs. This means taking a long-term view and considering our actions' environmental, social, and economic impacts.

In the tea industry, sustainability is a critical concern. Tea is the most widely consumed beverage in the world, second only to water. It is an important economic driver for many countries, particularly in the developing world. However, the production of tea is not without its challenges.

One of the key issues facing the tea industry is the impact of climate change. Tea plants are highly sensitive to changes in temperature and rainfall patterns, and the effects of global warming are already being felt in many tea-growing regions. In some areas, tea plants are struggling to cope with extreme heat and drought, while in others, heavy rainfall and flooding are causing serious damage to crops.

To address these challenges, many tea producers are adopting sustainable practices to protect their crops and ensure the long-term viability of their operations. This includes using more efficient irrigation systems, implementing water conservation measures, and planting more resilient varieties of tea plants.

Another key aspect of sustainability in the tea industry is the protection of the environment. Tea plants require a specific type of soil and climate to thrive, and the cultivation of tea can significantly impact the natural habitats of the regions in which it is grown. To minimize this impact, many tea producers use organic and natural farming methods, avoiding synthetic pesticides and fertilizers. This not only helps preserve the soil and water's health but also ensures that the tea produced is free from harmful chemicals.

In addition to environmental concerns, tea production's social and economic impacts must also be considered. Many tea workers live in rural areas, and their livelihoods depend on the tea industry. Supporting these workers and their communities is essential to ensure that tea production is sustainable. This includes providing fair wages, safe working conditions, and access to education and healthcare.

One way that tea producers support their workers is by implementing fair trade practices. Fairtrade is a global movement that promotes the rights of workers and farmers and ensures that they are paid a fair price for their products. This allows tea producers to provide better living conditions and support for their workers while also ensuring that they can sustain their operations in the long term.

Tea Leaves vs. Tea Bags

Tea leaves are often considered superior to tea bags for various reasons. For one, tea leaves provide a fuller, more complex flavor than tea bags. This is because tea leaves are made from the entire tea plant, while tea bags often contain only the dusty remnants of the tea plant known as "fannings" or "dust." As a result, tea leaves tend to have a richer, more nuanced flavor than tea bags.

Another reason tea leaves are preferable to tea bags is that they allow for greater control over the brewing process. With tea leaves, you can experiment with different steeping times and water temperatures to find the perfect cup of tea. This is not possible with tea bags, which are pre-portioned and pre-steeped, leaving little room for experimentation.

Furthermore, tea leaves are of greater quality than tea bags because tea leaves are often produced from whole, high-quality tea leaves, whereas tea bags are frequently made from lower-quality tea leaves and other plant materials. As a result, tea leaves are more tasty and fresher than tea bags.

Furthermore, tea leaves are better for the environment than tea bags. Many tea bags are made from non-biodegradable materials, such as plastic, that can take hundreds of years to break down in the environment. In contrast, tea leaves are completely biodegradable and do not pose the same environmental risks as tea bags.

Overall, tea leaves are preferable to tea bags for their fuller flavor, greater control over the brewing process, higher quality, and environmental benefits. While tea bags may be convenient, tea leaves offer a superior cup of tea that is well worth the extra effort.

The Five Most Expensive Teas on the Planet

The world of tea is vast and varied, with countless varieties and styles to choose from. Some of the most expensive teas in the world are highly sought after for their unique flavors and aromas, as well as their rarity and history. Here are five of the most expensive teas in the world, along with a brief description of each one.

Tie Guan Yin Tea

This type of tea, also known as Iron Goddess of Mercy tea, is a highly prized variety of oolong tea from the Anxi region of China's Fujian province. It is named after the Chinese goddess Guan Yin and is known for its complex and floral flavor profile, with hints of honey, fruit, and orchid. Tie Guan Yin tea is often aged for several years before being sold, contributing to its high price.

Gyokuro Tea

This type of Japanese green tea is grown in the shade, which produces a unique flavor profile that is rich and vegetal with a slightly sweet finish. Gyokuro tea leaves are carefully hand-picked and processed using techniques that have been refined over centuries.

Da-Hong Pao Tea

Another highly prized oolong tea from China, Da-Hong Pao is known for its bold and complex flavor, with hints of dark chocolate and roasted nuts. The tea is named after a group of six tea bushes that are said to have miraculous healing powers and are grown in the Wuyi Mountains of China's Fujian province. The high price of Da-Hong Pao tea is due to its limited availability and the demanding production process, which involves roasting the leaves multiple times to develop their flavor.

Pu-erh Tea

Pu-erh tea is produced in the Yunnan province of China and has a long history dating back to the Tang Dynasty. This type of tea is made from fermented and aged tea leaves and is known for its earthy and mellow flavor.

White Peony Tea

White Peony tea is grown in the Fujian province of China and is carefully hand-picked and processed to preserve its delicate flavor and aroma. This type of white tea is made from the tea plant's young leaves and unopened buds and is known for its soothing and floral flavor. The high price of White Peony tea is due to its rarity and the labor-intensive production process, as well as its delicate flavor and health benefits.

The Proper Way to Store Tea

Storing tea leaves properly is essential to maintaining their freshness and flavor. Tea leaves are delicate and can easily lose their flavor and aroma if not stored properly. Proper storage can also help prevent the growth of bacteria and other contaminants that can spoil the tea.

It is critical to keep tea leaves away from heat, light, moisture, and strong odors when storing them. This means keeping them in a cool, dry, and dark place, such as a pantry or cupboard. Avoid storing tea near heat-producing appliances such as ovens, stoves, and radiators, as well as windows and places with direct sunlight.

It's also essential to keep tea leaves in an airtight container to prevent them from drying out or absorbing moisture and odors from the air. Glass containers with tight-fitting lids are ideal for storing tea leaves, as they are opaque and protect the tea from light. Avoid using plastic containers, as they can release chemicals that affect the tea's flavor.

When it comes to the type of tea, loose-leaf teas are the most delicate and require the most careful storage. Loose leaf teas should be stored in small, airtight containers and only kept in larger containers when ready to brew. This will prevent the tea leaves from being crushed and losing their flavor and aroma.

Different teas have different flavors and aromas, and keeping them together can result in the flavors and aromas mixing and affecting each other. This is especially important for teas with intense flavors, such as black tea and oolong tea.

To further protect the tea leaves, it's also a good idea to store them in the refrigerator or freezer. Doing so will slow down the oxidation process and preserve the flavor and aroma of the tea leaves for longer. However, keep the tea leaves in an airtight container to avoid absorbing moisture and odors from the fridge or freezer.

Also, remember to properly label and date the containers. This will help you keep track of the tea leaves and ensure you use the freshest tea possible. It's also a good idea to use the tea leaves within six months to a year of purchasing them to always enjoy the best flavor and aroma.

Chapter Two

The Hidden Health Benefits of Tea

Drinking a good cup of tea is a comforting and delightful experience that can provide numerous positive health effects. These benefits of tea are attributed to the presence of various bioactive compounds such as polyphenols, catechins, and flavonoids, which are potent antioxidants that help to protect cells from damage caused by free radicals.

Here are seven reasons why you should make drinking tea a part of your daily routine:

Tea Boost Immune System

Inflammation is the body's natural response to protect itself from harm, such as an injury or infection. However, chronic inflammation can lead to various health issues, such as heart disease, arthritis, and even cancer. Fortunately, tea can help combat inflammation and reduce the risk of these health issues.

Tea contains a variety of antioxidants and polyphenols, which are compounds that have anti-inflammatory properties. These compounds can help reduce the levels of inflammatory markers in the body, decreasing chronic inflammation. Green tea, in particular, is known for its high levels of these compounds and has been shown to have anti-inflammatory effects.

In addition to reducing inflammation, tea can also help boost your immune system. The antioxidants and polyphenols in tea can help support the immune system, protecting the body from harmful bacteria and viruses. By strengthening the immune system and enhancing its ability to fight off invading pathogens, these compounds can help minimize the risk of infection.

Not all teas are created equal when it comes to their health benefits. Black tea, green tea, and white tea are the most common types of tea, and all have different levels of antioxidants and polyphenols. Black tea is the most processed type of tea and therefore has the lowest levels of these compounds. Green tea, on the other hand, is minimally processed and has higher levels of antioxidants and polyphenols, making it the most beneficial for reducing inflammation and boosting the immune system. White tea is the least processed type of tea and also has high levels of these compounds, making it an excellent choice for health benefits.

The way it is brewed can also affect its health benefits. For the best results, it is recommended to brew tea with hot water (not boiling) for 3-5 minutes. This allows for the release of antioxidants and polyphenols into the water, making them more readily available for the body to absorb.

Tea Improves Heart Health

One of the key benefits of tea is its ability to improve heart health.

The heart is a vital organ in the human body and is responsible for pumping blood to the rest of the body. It is essential to maintain good heart health as it can help prevent various health conditions such as heart disease and stroke.

Tea is rich in antioxidants, which are compounds that help protect the body from harmful free radicals. These free radicals can cause damage to cells and lead to chronic diseases such as heart disease. By consuming tea, you can help reduce the levels of free radicals in your body and protect your heart from potential risks.

Green tea, in particular, is beneficial for heart health. It contains a high amount of catechins, an antioxidant linked to lower cholesterol levels and improved blood flow. Green tea has also been shown to lower the risk of developing heart disease and stroke.

Tea also includes flavonoids in addition to antioxidants. These plant-based components have been proven to improve heart health by lowering blood pressure and reducing the risk of blood clots.

Tea can also help reduce inflammation in the body when consumed regularly. Chronic inflammation is linked to a higher risk of heart disease and other health conditions. Drinking tea can help lower inflammation and boost your overall heart health.

Moreover, drinking tea can positively impact your mental health. Tea has been shown to help reduce stress and improve cognitive function, which can positively impact heart health.

It is important to note that not all teas are created equal. It is important to choose high-quality teas that are free of additives and chemicals. Organic teas are a great option as they are grown without harmful pesticides and chemicals.

Tea Helps with Weight Loss

Tea has long been recognized for its numerous health benefits, including its ability to help with weight loss. Many people are unaware of tea's possible weight loss benefits, but studies have shown that it can be an excellent tool in the fight against bulges.

First and foremost, tea contains several natural compounds that can boost metabolism and help the body burn more calories. One of the most well-known compounds is caffeine, which is found in green and black tea. Caffeine stimulates the central nervous system and increases the body's ability to burn fat, leading to increased weight loss.

In addition to its fat-burning properties, tea includes antioxidants called catechins, which can help the body break down fat cells and prevent them from developing. Green tea, in particular, is high in catechins and can help you lose weight.

Another way that tea can help with weight loss is by suppressing the appetite. Many people turn to food as a way to cope with stress or boredom, but drinking tea can help curb those cravings and keep you from reaching for unhealthy snacks. The act of sipping on a warm cup of tea can also provide a sense of relaxation and calm, which can help reduce stress eating.

Of course, it's important to remember that drinking tea alone won't magically make the pounds disappear. A balanced diet and regular exercise are still necessary to achieve significant weight loss. However, incorporating tea into a healthy lifestyle can provide an added boost and help support your weight loss efforts.

Tea Promotes Mental and Emotional Wellbeing

As I mentioned previously, modern research has shown that tea contains several compounds that can positively impact our mental and emotional well-being.

One of the key reasons why tea can help boost mood and reduce stress is its high content of antioxidants. As we already know, these powerful compounds help to protect our cells from damage caused by free radicals, which are unstable molecules that can cause inflammation and other harmful effects in the body. By neutralizing these free radicals, antioxidants help to keep our cells healthy and functioning correctly.

One of the most well-known antioxidants found in tea is called epigallocatechin gallate, or EGCG for short. This chemical is present in high amounts in green tea and has been proven to offer a wide range of health benefits. It has been found, for example, to help protect against heart disease and cancer and boost cognitive function and memory.

In addition to its high content of antioxidants, tea also contains some other compounds that can help to improve mood and reduce stress. For example, it contains caffeine, which is a stimulant that can help to increase alertness and focus. However, unlike other sources of caffeine, such as coffee, tea contains lower levels of this compound, meaning that it is less likely to cause jitteriness or other negative side effects.

Another key compound found in tea is L-theanine, which is an amino acid that is unique to tea plants. This compound has been shown to significantly benefit the brain, improving mood and reducing stress. For example, studies have shown that L-theanine can help to increase levels of the neurotransmitter GABA, which is responsible for calming the brain and promoting relaxation.

Drinking tea has also been linked to a variety of additional health benefits. For example, it can help improve digestion, reduce bloating, and promote healthy weight loss. In addition, it can help improve oral health and prevent tooth decay, thanks to its high fluoride content.

Tea Stimulates Oral Health

Bad breath, also known as halitosis, is a common issue caused by various factors, including poor oral hygiene, certain medications, and underlying medical conditions. It can be embarrassing and affect one's self-confidence and social interactions.

Fortunately, drinking tea can be a natural and effective way to combat bad breath. Here are a few reasons why:

- Tea contains antioxidants that fight bacteria. Tea leaves, particularly green and black tea, contain polyphenols, an antioxidant shown to have antibacterial properties. These antioxidants can help eliminate the bacteria in the mouth that contribute to bad breath.

- Tea can help neutralize odor-causing compounds. When we eat some foods, they release certain chemicals that can cause bad breath. Tea, particularly green tea, can help neutralize these compounds, reducing their odor-causing potential.

- Tea can stimulate saliva production. Saliva is essential for maintaining a healthy mouth as it helps wash away food particles and bacteria. Tea, mainly black tea, can stimulate saliva production, which can help reduce bad breath.

- Tea can help improve overall oral hygiene. Good oral hygiene is essential for preventing bad breath. Tea, particularly green tea, has some antimicrobial properties that can help reduce the growth of bacteria in the mouth. This, in turn, can help improve overall oral hygiene and reduce bad breath.

Drinking tea can also provide other oral health benefits, such as reducing the risk of cavities and gum diseases.

It's important to note that while tea can help reduce bad breath, it should not be relied on as the sole solution. Proper oral hygiene, including brushing and flossing daily, is still essential. Additionally, if bad breath persists, it's important to consult a healthcare provider to determine the underlying causes and appropriate treatment.

Tea Improves Brain Function

Did you know that tea can also improve brain function?

It's true! Regular tea consumption has been linked to increased cognitive performance, enhanced concentration, and improved memory.

One of the key components in tea that contributes to these brain-boosting effects is a group of natural plant compounds called flavonoids. These powerful antioxidants are found in many different types of tea, including green, black, and white tea, and improve blood flow to the brain.

Improved blood flow to the brain means more oxygen and nutrients are delivered to the cells, which can help them function more efficiently. This can result in increased mental clarity, focus, and overall brain health.

Another benefit of tea is its ability to reduce stress and anxiety. The combination of caffeine and theanine, an amino acid found in tea leaves, has been demonstrated in studies to have a calming effect on the mind. This can help improve mood and reduce feelings of stress and anxiety, which can negatively impact brain function.

Regular consumption has also been linked to a reduced risk of developing neurode-generative diseases such as Alzheimer's and Parkinson's. The antioxidants found in tea have been shown to protect brain cells from damage, which can help to prevent these conditions from developing.

So, next time you reach for a cup of tea, remember that it's not just a tasty beverage – it's also good for your brain! So go ahead, pour yourself a cup and let the brain-boosting effects of tea help you stay focused and on top of your game.

Tea May Help Prevent and Manage Type 2 Diabetes

Drinking tea has other health benefits, such as the potential to prevent or manage diabetes.

Diabetes is a chronic condition that occurs when the body is unable to properly regulate blood sugar levels. There are two main types of diabetes: type 1 and type 2. Type 1 diabetes is an autoimmune disease in which the body's immune system attacks and destroys the cells in the pancreas that produce insulin. Type 2 diabetes, on the other hand, is a metabolic disorder characterized by high blood sugar levels, insulin resistance, and a relative lack of insulin.

Both types of diabetes can lead to serious health complications, such as heart disease, nerve damage, and kidney damage. However, type 2 diabetes is more common and often develops later in life due to poor diet and lifestyle choices.

One way to prevent or manage diabetes is to make lifestyle changes, such as eating a healthy diet and exercising regularly. Another potential way to prevent or manage the condition is by drinking tea.

Tea, especially green tea, has been shown to have several health benefits. It is rich in antioxidants, which can help protect the body against damage from free radicals. Free radicals are unstable molecules that can cause damage to cells, leading to various health problems. By neutralizing free radicals, antioxidants can help protect the body against diseases like diabetes.

Green tea can have anti-inflammatory effects. Inflammation is a normal immune response that occurs when the body is trying to fight off an infection or injury. However, chronic inflammation can contribute to developing diseases such as diabetes. By reducing inflammation, green tea may help prevent or manage the condition.

CHAPTER THREE
Tea Culture Around the World

Tea is a popular beverage worldwide and has a long history of being an important part of many different cultures and countries. In this chapter, I'd like to take you on a journey throughout the world and introduce you to tea culture.

English Afternoon Tea

Afternoon tea, also known as "low tea," is a cherished tradition in England. It originated in the early 19th century as a way for the upper class to stave off hunger between lunch and dinner. The practice quickly became popular among the social elite and eventually spread to the rest of society.

The traditional English afternoon tea consists of a selection of sandwiches, scones with clotted cream and jam, and pastries; all served with a pot of tea. The sandwiches typically include cucumber, egg and cress, and smoked salmon, while the scones are served warm, and the pastries may include fruit tarts and éclairs.

Afternoon tea is typically served in the late afternoon, between 3 and 5 pm. It is often held in a drawing room or parlor, with guests seated at small tables and served by waitstaff. The tea is brewed in a teapot and poured into individual cups, with milk and sugar offered on the side.

The ritual of afternoon tea is steeped in tradition and etiquette. It is considered rude to clink teacups or to make noise while eating delicate sandwiches and pastries. The tea should be poured for others before oneself, and the sandwiches and pastries are to be eaten in a specific order, starting with the savory sandwiches and ending with the sweet pastries.

In recent years, afternoon tea has become a popular tourist attraction in England, with many hotels and restaurants offering their own unique twists on the classic tradition. Some offer champagne or other beverages in addition to tea, and some feature exotic teas from around the world.

Despite its origins as a social event for the upper class, afternoon tea has become a beloved tradition for all members of English society. It is a time to relax, socialize, and enjoy the finer things in life, all while savoring the comforting warmth of a cup of tea.

Chinese Cha-Dao

Cha-dao, or the "Way of Tea," is a centuries-old tradition in Chinese culture that centers around the preparation and enjoyment of tea. The art of cha-dao has evolved over time and has greatly influenced tea-drinking customs in other parts of the world.

The origins of cha-dao can be traced back to the Tang Dynasty (618-907 AD) when tea was first introduced to China from neighboring countries. At the time, tea was considered to have medicinal properties and was used in religious ceremonies. Over time, tea became more widely consumed, and the art of preparing and drinking tea became a highly refined and respected practice.

One of the key principles of cha-dao is the focus on the quality and presentation of the tea itself. Chinese tea masters, known as chajin, spend years learning the art of tea preparation and are highly skilled in selecting the best leaves, water, and utensils for brewing the perfect cup of tea.

The traditional method of preparing tea in cha-dao involves using a small teapot, called a yixing pot, to brew the tea leaves. The yixing pot is made from a porous clay that absorbs the flavor of the tea and is, therefore, only used for brewing a single type of tea. The tea leaves are rinsed in hot water to cleanse them and enhance their flavor. The water is then discarded, and the tea leaves are steeped in freshly boiled water for a few minutes before being served.

The tea is typically served in small cups, and each person is served one cup at a time. The tea is then poured from the teapot into the cup, and the process is repeated until each person has been served. This ritual is believed to foster a sense of harmony and respect among tea drinkers.

In addition to the traditional methods of preparing and serving tea, cha-dao also includes a range of tea-related customs and rituals. For example, tea gardens are often considered sacred spaces where tea plants are grown and harvested. Tea ceremonies, where tea is prepared and served according to strict rules, are also a key part of cha-dao.

Indian Chai

 Indian chai, or tea as it is commonly known, has a rich history and cultural significance in the country. It is a beloved beverage consumed by millions on a daily basis, and its origins can be traced back to ancient times.

The origins of Indian chai can be traced back to the ancient Ayurvedic practice of mixing herbs and spices with hot water to create a therapeutic and nourishing drink. Over time, this practice evolved into the use of tea leaves, which were introduced to India by the British during the colonial era.

Since then, chai has become an integral part of Indian culture and is consumed by people from all walks of life. It is a popular beverage that is enjoyed at all times of the day, from morning breakfast to evening snacks.

Chai has become such an integral part of Indian culture that it is often referred to as the country's national drink. It is consumed by people from all walks of life, from the wealthy to the poor, and is considered an essential element of many social gatherings and occasions.

The popularity of chai in India has also led to the development of a wide variety of chai blends and flavors. From the classic masala chai, made with a mixture of spices like cardamom, cinnamon, and cloves, to the more exotic flavors like ginger and saffron, there is a chai blend to suit every taste and preference. Love of chai in India has also led to the emergence of a vibrant chai culture, with chai shops and stalls found on every street corner. These chai shops serve as important social hubs, where people come together to enjoy a cup of chai and catch up with friends and family.

In addition to its cultural significance, chai also has numerous health benefits. The herbs and spices used in chai have medicinal properties that can help to boost the immune system and improve digestion.

Russian Samovars

Russian samovars are traditional metal teapots that have been used in Russian tea culture for centuries. These beautifully crafted teapots are known for their intricate designs and elegant shape and have long been a staple of Russian tea culture.

The origins of the Russian samovar can be traced back to the 18th century when tea was first introduced to Russia. At that time, tea was a luxury item that was only affordable to the wealthy and was often served at lavish banquets and other social gatherings.

To prepare the tea, a samovar was used to heat water to boiling. The tea leaves were then placed in a small metal teapot called a "samovarik," which was placed inside the larger samovar. Once the water was boiling, it was poured over the tea leaves, allowing it to steep for several minutes. The resulting tea was strong and rich and was often served with sugar, lemon, and other sweeteners to enhance its flavor. Samovars were also often decorated with intricate designs and patterns, making them popular for displaying in the home.

In addition to their practical use, Russian samovars also played a significant role in Russian social life. In the 19th century, they became a common sight in Russian tea rooms, where people would gather to enjoy tea and socialize.

Samovars were also often used as a symbol of hospitality and generosity, with hosts offering tea to guests as a sign of generosity and goodwill. As a result, Russian samovars became an integral part of Russian tea culture and remained a popular choice for preparing and serving tea to this day. Russian samovars are still widely used in Russia and can be found in many homes and tea rooms throughout the country. They are also a popular choice for collectors, with many people displaying these beautiful teapots in their homes as a reminder of Russian tea culture and tradition.

Tibetan Butter Tea

Tibetan butter tea, also known as po cha, is a traditional beverage enjoyed in Tibet for centuries. It is made by blending tea leaves with yak butter, salt, and water to create a rich, creamy beverage that is both nourishing and warming.

The origins of Tibetan butter tea can be traced back to the nomadic herders of Tibet, who needed a high-calorie drink to sustain them in the harsh, cold climate of the Himalayan plateau. The tea leaves and yak butter provided them with the necessary nutrients to keep their bodies fueled and warm, and the addition of salt helped to replenish the electrolytes lost through sweat and exertion.

Over time, the preparation of Tibetan butter tea has become a ritual and a central part of Tibetan culture. The tea is typically brewed in a large wooden kettle, using a wooden churn to mix the ingredients together. The resulting beverage is thick and frothy, with a rich, savory flavor that is unlike any other tea in the world.

Many Tibetans start their day with a cup of butter tea, which is often served to guests as a sign of hospitality. In addition to its nutritional value, Tibetan butter tea is also thought to have medicinal properties. It is believed to aid digestion, boost the immune system, and improve overall health.

Butter tea is not well-known outside of the region despite its popularity in Tibet. Many people find the idea of adding butter to tea to be strange and unappealing. However, those who have tried Tibetan butter tea often find it surprisingly delicious. So, it is worth trying if you are ever in the region.

Moroccan Mint Tea

Moroccan mint tea, also known as Moroccan green tea or simply "mint tea," is a staple of Moroccan culture and hospitality. The tea is made by brewing green tea leaves with fresh mint leaves and sugar, resulting in a sweet and refreshing drink that is often served to guests as a sign of hospitality.

Traditionally, Moroccan mint tea is made in a tall, narrow-necked teapot called a "berrad," heated over a gas or charcoal stove. The tea leaves and mint are placed in the pot, along with a generous amount of sugar. The pot is then filled with boiling water and left to steep for several minutes until the tea is a deep, rich green color.

Once the tea is ready, it is poured into small glasses from a height of several feet, creating a frothy head on the tea. This pouring technique is an essential part of the tea-making process and is said to help mix the ingredients and release the tea's flavor.

Moroccan mint tea is typically served with a tray of small sweets or pastries, which are enjoyed alongside the tea. The tea is often poured by the head of the household or the group's most senior member and is ceremonially served to guests.

In addition to being a popular beverage, Moroccan mint tea also has cultural and social significance. The ritual of preparing and serving the tea is an important part of Moroccan life, and the tea itself is seen as a symbol of hospitality and good manners.

In many Moroccan households, mint tea is a daily staple enjoyed throughout the day, not just as a formal gesture of hospitality. It is also common at Moroccan markets and street vendors, where it is often served hot and sweet to thirsty shoppers.

Despite its popularity, Moroccan mint tea is not just a local phenomenon. This tea has gained popularity worldwide in recent years and can now be found in many international cafes and restaurants. Its unique flavor and ritual preparation make it a fascinating and delicious part of Moroccan culture.

Iranian Teahouses

Iranian teahouses, also known as "chaykhaneh", have been a staple of Persian culture for centuries. These establishments serve as a gathering place for friends and family to socialize, discuss current events, and enjoy a cup of tea.

The tradition of teahouses can be traced back to the Safavid Dynasty in the 16th century when the Persian ruler Shah Abbas I introduced the practice of drinking tea to Iran. Before, tea was mainly consumed by the elite and considered a luxury item. However, with the introduction of tea plantations and the growth of the tea trade, it became more accessible to the general population.

Teahouses quickly became popular gathering places for both men and women. In traditional Iranian culture, men and women are often segregated in public spaces, but teahouses were one of the few places where both genders could interact and socialize.

The interior of a typical Iranian teahouse is adorned with intricate designs and colorful decorations. The walls are often adorned with complex tile work, and the floors are covered with Persian carpets. The seating arrangement usually comprises low tables and cushions, allowing for a comfortable and relaxed atmosphere.

Tea is typically served in small glasses, accompanied by a bowl of sugar crystals to sweeten the drink. In addition to tea, teahouses also serve a variety of snacks and pastries. Traditional Iranian snacks such as "lavashak" (fruit leather), baklava, and "gaz" (a type of nougat) can often be found on the menu.

Iranian teahouses are not just places to enjoy a perpetrator: many are also used as a place of business. It is not uncommon to see people conducting meetings or negotiations over a cup of tea in a teahouse. In fact, some teahouses even have private rooms available for such occasions.

One of the most famous teahouses in Iran is the Narenjestan-e Qavam in Shiraz. Built in the 19th century, this teahouse is known for its beautiful gardens and intricate design. It has even been declared a national heritage site.

Despite their popularity, Iranian teahouses have faced challenges in recent years. In 2010, the government implemented a ban on smoking in public places, which included teahouses. This caused a significant decrease in business for many teahouses, as smoking and tea drinking go hand in hand in Iranian culture.

However, the tradition of the Iranian teahouse continues to thrive. They remain an important part of Iranian culture, providing a space for socialization and relaxation. Whether enjoying a cup of tea with friends or conducting business, the Iranian teahouse will always hold a special place in the hearts of Iranians.

Thai Iced Tea

Thai iced tea, also known as "cha yen" in Thai, is a popular and beloved beverage in Thailand. It is made from strongly-brewed black tea, sweetened with sugar and condensed milk, and poured over ice.

The origins of Thai iced tea can be traced back to the late 19th century when tea was introduced to Thailand by Chinese immigrants. Initially, tea was mostly consumed by the wealthy and elite in Thailand, but it quickly gained popularity among all social classes.

One of the key ingredients in Thai iced tea is the type of black tea used. In Thailand, a special type of black tea called "cha thong" is used. This tea has a distinctive orange color and is known for its bold, robust flavor. It is often blended with other herbs and spices, such as star anise, tamarind, and vanilla, to give it a unique and flavorful taste.

In order to make Thai iced tea, the tea leaves are first brewed in boiling water for several minutes to extract the flavor. The brewed tea is then strained and sweetened with sugar and condensed milk, which gives it a creamy and rich flavor. The sweetened tea is then poured over ice and served in a tall glass.

In Thailand, Thai iced tea is often served with a variety of sweet snacks and desserts, such as sugary doughnuts, sweet pancakes, and sticky rice. It is also commonly served with spicy dishes, as the tea's sweetness helps balance out the spices' heat.

Thai iced tea has become popular around the world and can be found in many Thai restaurants and cafes. It is typically served in a tall glass with a thick layer of foam on top and garnished with a sprig of fresh mint or a slice of orange.

In addition to its delicious taste, Thai iced tea is also known for its beautiful color. The vibrant orange color of the tea is often admired and appreciated by those who try it.

Japanese Tea Ceremony

The Japanese tea ceremony, also known as the Way of Tea, is a traditional ritual in Japanese culture that centers around preparing and enjoying green tea, known as matcha. The tea ceremony originated in China, but the Japanese developed it into the refined and elaborate ritual that it is today.

The tea ceremony is more than just a simple social event – it is a spiritual and aesthetic practice that seeks to bring about a sense of inner peace and harmony. The ceremony is steeped in symbolism, and every aspect of the ritual, from the choice of tea to the design of the tea room, has a deep cultural and philosophical meaning.

One of the key principles of the tea ceremony is the concept of ichi-go ichi-e, which roughly translates to "one time, one meeting." This principle emphasizes the importance of being present in the moment and appreciating the uniqueness of each tea ceremony, as it will never be repeated in the same way.

The tea ceremony is typically held in a tea room, known as a chashitsu. These rooms are designed to be simple and unadorned, with a minimalist aesthetic that reflects the tea master's humility and respect for the tea. The tea room is typically small, with tatami mat flooring and sliding paper screens called fusuma that can be opened to allow natural light into the room.

The tea ceremony begins with the guests seated on cushions in a line facing the tokonoma, an alcove in the tea room where a flower arrangement, calligraphy scroll, or other decorative object is displayed. The host, known as the tea master, enters the room and performs a ceremonial purification ritual known as temae. This involves washing and rinsing the utensils and tea bowl and carefully preparing the tea using precise measurements and movements.

Once the tea is prepared, the tea master offers a bowl of tea to the most honored guest, who takes a sip and passes the bowl to the next guest. The guests are expected to appreciate the tea and the ceremony with all of their senses, taking in the aroma, flavor, and appearance of the tea as well as the ambiance of the tea room.

The tea ceremony is more than just about the tea itself, as it is a complex cultural practice that involves specific rituals, gestures, and etiquette. The tea ceremony is an opportunity for participants to slow down, connect with others, and appreciate the moment's beauty. It is a form of meditation and a way to cultivate mindfulness and awareness.

Argentinian Yerba Mate

Argentinian Yerba Mate is a traditional South American herbal tea that has been enjoyed for centuries by the indigenous people of Argentina, Uruguay, and Paraguay. It is made from the leaves of the Ilex paraguariensis plant, which is native to the region and has been used for medicinal and spiritual purposes for thousands of years.

The preparation of Yerba Mate involves steeping the dried leaves in hot water and drinking the resulting infusion through a metal straw called a bombilla, which is traditionally made from silver or brass. The tea is typically served in a gourd, called a calabash, and is consumed communally, with friends and family sharing the same gourd and bombilla.

The popularity of Yerba Mate has spread beyond its traditional cultural roots and is now enjoyed by people from all walks of life in Argentina and beyond. It is known for its stimulating and energizing effects, which are attributed to the plant's high caffeine content and its high levels of vitamins and minerals.

One of the most notable health benefits of Yerba Mate is its ability to improve mental clarity and focus. The tea contains a unique blend of caffeine, theophylline, and theobromine, which work together to provide a smooth, sustained energy boost without the jittery side effects commonly associated with coffee. This makes it a great alternative for those who are sensitive to caffeine or want a more balanced energy boost.

Yerba Mate is also rich in antioxidants, which can help protect against the damaging effects of free radicals in the body. These antioxidants are believed to have anti-inflammatory properties, which can help reduce the risk of chronic diseases such as cancer, heart disease, and diabetes.

In addition to its health benefits, Yerba Mate is also a rich source of vitamins and minerals. It contains vitamins A, C, E, and B-complex and calcium, potassium, and magnesium. This makes it a great addition to any healthy diet and a perfect choice for those looking to increase their intake of essential nutrients.

The traditional preparation of Yerba Mate is an important part of Argentine culture, and the tea is often consumed during social gatherings and special occasions. In Argentina, it is not uncommon to see people carrying a gourd and bombilla with them wherever they go, ready to share a cup of Yerba Mate with friends and family.

The popularity of Yerba Mate has grown in recent years, and it is now widely available in stores and online. It can be purchased in loose-leaf form or in tea bags and is also available in a variety of flavors, including traditional, mint, and fruit-flavored blends.

Taiwanese Bubble Tea

Taiwanese Bubble Tea, also known as pearl milk tea or boba tea, is a delicious and refreshing drink that originated in Taiwan in the 1980s. This sweet and creamy beverage has become a global phenomenon, with bubble tea shops popping up all over the world.

Bubble tea is made by mixing brewed tea with a sweetener and milk or cream. The distinctive bubbles, or "pearls," are made from tapioca starch and added to the drink. The pearls add a chewy texture and a burst of sweetness to the drink.

There are many variations of bubble tea, including green tea, black tea, and oolong tea. The sweetener and milk can also be varied to create different flavors and textures. Some popular bubble tea flavors include mango, strawberry, and coconut.

Bubble tea is typically served with a large straw, allowing the pearls to be easily sipped up and enjoyed. The drink is often served cold but can also be enjoyed hot during the colder months.

The popularity of bubble tea has exploded in recent years, with bubble tea shops popping up worldwide. In Taiwan, bubble tea is often seen as a cultural icon, with many locals drinking it daily. The drink is also popular among tourists, who are drawn to its unique flavor and texture.

There are many theories as to why bubble tea has become so popular. Some believe that it is the chewy texture of the pearls that makes the drink so appealing. Others argue that the variety of flavors and customizable options make it a hit.

Regardless of the reasons, bubble tea continues to grow in popularity and is a beloved drink among many people around the world. Whether you are a tea lover, a lover of sweet and creamy drinks, or simply looking for something new and exciting to try, bubble tea is definitely worth a sip.

Turkish Chai

Turkish Chai, also known as çay, is a staple beverage in Turkey and surrounding countries. It is a black tea that is brewed with loose tea leaves and served in small glasses.

The origins of Turkish Chai can be traced back to the Ottoman Empire, where Chinese traders first introduced it. The tea quickly became a popular beverage among the Ottoman elite and soon spread throughout the empire.

The preparation of Turkish Chai is an art form in itself. The tea leaves are carefully selected and blended to create the perfect flavor. The tea is then brewed in a traditional Turkish teapot called a çaydanlık, with a long spout for pouring the tea into the small glasses.

When drinking Turkish Chai, it is customary to add sugar to the tea. The amount of sugar added can vary depending on personal preference, but it is typically served with a generous amount.

In Turkish culture, Turkish Chai is not just a beverage but a social activity. It is often served in tea houses, where friends and family gather to catch up and enjoy the tea together. It is also a common offering when visiting someone's home as a sign of hospitality.

In recent years, Turkish Chai has gained more popularity outside of Turkey and can be found in many cafes and restaurants worldwide. While the traditional preparation method is still highly regarded, many variations of Turkish Chai are also available, such as spiced chai or chai lattes.

The Tea Party, a centuries-old tradition steeped in British culture, has been a popular social event for many years. Whether you are a seasoned pro or new to the world of tea parties, it is essential to follow proper etiquette to ensure everyone has an enjoyable experience. Let's discuss some key aspects of Tea Party etiquette, including what to wear, behave, and properly prepare and serve tea.

First and foremost, it is important to consider what to wear to a Tea Party. While there is no strict dress code, it is generally regarded as polite to dress in a manner that is appropriate for the occasion. For a more formal Tea Party, men may wish to wear a suit and tie, while women may opt for a dress or skirt and blouse. For a less formal Tea Party, smart casual attire is usually acceptable.

Once you have decided on your outfit, it is time to focus on your behavior at the Tea Party. As with any social gathering, it is essential to be respectful and considerate of others. This means being polite and gracious, attentively listening when others are speaking, and avoiding inappropriate or offensive topics of conversation. It is also important to be mindful of your body language and to maintain good posture, as this can affect the overall atmosphere of the Tea Party.

When it comes to preparing and serving tea, there are a few key rules to follow. First, make sure that the tea is brewed at the correct temperature and for the right amount of time, as this can greatly affect the taste and flavor of the tea. Using fresh, high-quality tea leaves and clean and properly prepared utensils is also important. Additionally, be sure to serve the tea in appropriate cups and saucers and to offer milk, sugar, and other accompaniments as desired.

In conclusion, Tea Party etiquette is all about being respectful, considerate, and mindful of others. By following these guidelines, you can help ensure that everyone has a pleasant experience at your Tea Party. Whether you are hosting or attending, the key is to be gracious, polite, and attentive and to take care in preparing and serving the tea. With these tips in mind, you can be confident in your ability to navigate the world of Tea Party etiquette with ease and grace.

Tea Museums Around the World

Tea museums are two popular tourist attractions that travelers love to visit. These destinations offer a unique blend of history, culture, and nature, making them ideal places to relax and unwind. Here are some of the most famous tea gardens and museums that you should consider visiting on your next vacation.

Tenfu Tea Museum, Zhangzhou, Fujian, China – For a genuine appreciation of the rich history and allure of tea, the province of Fujian is a must-visit destination. Known as the birthplace of numerous significant tea varieties, Fujian abounds with historical tea narratives, expansive tea bush fields, quaint tea shops, and the world's largest tea museum — the Tenfu Tea Museum. This extraordinary museum provides a multitude of experiences for the tea connoisseur — a main exhibit hall narrating the historical journey of tea, a tea tasting room for flavor exploration, a room dedicated to calligraphy and Chinese painting, and a Japanese tea room for a taste of international tea culture.

Pinglin Tea Museum, New Taipei, Taiwan – Taiwanese tea enthusiasts must consider adding the Pinglin Tea Museum to their list of must-visit tea destinations. Renowned for its prestigious Baozhong oolong tea, Pinglin serves as an important center for this much-loved Taiwanese brew. With four distinct sections - the main Exhibition Hall, Tea Art Hall, Multimedia Hall, and Theme Hall - the museum provides visitors with a comprehensive understanding of Chinese tea, touching upon its history, production processes, and brewing techniques among other fascinating aspects.

Ceylon Tea Museum, Hantana, Sri Lanka – Situated near Kandy, the city where tea cultivation first began in Sri Lanka, the Ceylon Tea Museum stands as one of the most significant tea museums in all of South Asia. Spread across two floors, the museum exhibits an extensive collection of tea-related machinery and artifacts, along with a well-stocked library. Furthermore, it also features a cafe and a shop, providing visitors with the opportunity to purchase the renowned Ceylon tea.

Happy Valley Tea Estate, Darjeeling, India – While Munnar's museum may hold the title of being the first, the factory at Happy Valley Tea Estate, perched at a height of 6800 ft in Darjeeling, boasts the distinction of being the loftiest. This tea garden holds a venerable position as the second-oldest in Darjeeling, a quaint town nestled in West Bengal. It's renowned for producing delectable black teas, carrying the signature muscatel flavor. The estate extends an invitation to a guided tour of their tea factory, offering a glimpse into the manufacturing process and the storied history of Darjeeling tea.

Tea Museum Shizuoka, Shimada, Shizuoka, Japan – Shizuoka holds a significant position as a major tea-producing region in Japan and hosts a remarkable Japanese tea museum that is a must-see for visitors. Apart from exploring the museum and immersing yourself in the history and culture of tea, there are additional attractions. You can revel in the serene ambiance of a tea ceremony house and garden, and even partake in interactive activities like tea plucking or grinding your own matcha.

Tea Room at the Boston Tea Party Museum - This museum is dedicated to the historical event that took place in Boston in 1773 when colonists threw tea into the harbor in protest of high taxes. The Tea Room at the museum offers a variety of teas and tea-themed desserts, as well as educational exhibits on the history of tea in the United States.

Gorreana Tea Museum, Sao Miguel, Azores, Portugal – Located in the heart of the Atlantic Ocean, the Azores is a Portuguese chain of islands that houses Gorreana, the oldest tea plantation in Europe. Gorreana continues to produce tea to this day and warmly welcomes tea enthusiasts who venture to the Azores. Here, you can meander through rows of lush tea bushes, delve into the intricacies of tea-making machinery, unwind with a soothing cup of European black or green tea, and gain deeper insights into the art of tea production.

Cutty Sark, London, England, UK – For those seeking to delve deeper into the history of European tea, a trip to the Cutty Sark is essential. This historic vessel is the final British tea clipper, specifically crafted to transport tea and other commodities from China. It stands as the sole surviving tea clipper that is not only preserved in remarkable condition but has been transformed into a museum, remaining open to the public for exploration.

Twinings Tea Museum, London, England, UK – Boasting a storied history that spans over three centuries, the Twinings Flagship store holds the distinction of being London's most time-honored tea shop. As one would expect, it also hosts a quaint tea museum in honor of Thomas Twining, the visionary behind this renowned British tea enterprise. Visitors can immerse themselves in the world of tea through unique experiences and master classes that the store offers.

Jeju Osulloc Tea Museum, Jeju, South Korea – When venturing to Jeju, a picturesque Korean island renowned for its tea, ensure you take the opportunity to explore the architecturally striking Jeju Tea Museum nestled close to the island's tea fields. It's not just a showcase for a unique collection of tea cups, but also offers a window into the captivating tradition of Korean tea. Furthermore, the museum houses a tea roasting room and displays an extensive assortment of tea cups from all corners of the globe.

Treasured Teapot Museum, New South Wales, Australia – For those with a keen interest in teapots, Bygone Beautys Treasured Teapot Museum is an ideal destination. With an astonishing assortment of over 5500 teapots, spanning from ancient to modern, traditional to contemporary, and sourced from all over the globe, it's a sight to behold. And if the sight of all these teapots kindles a desire for a brew, you're in luck. The museum also hosts a quaint tearoom where you can indulge in a classic high tea experience.

CHAPTER FOUR

The Five Main Types of Tea

As you know by now, tea has a long history and many different kinds, so it has a wide range of tastes, smells, and health benefits. From mild white tea to strong black tea, there is a type of tea for every taste. If you don't know much about tea, the many different kinds and varieties may be hard to understand and scary. In this chapter, we'll discuss the different kinds of tea and what makes them unique.

Black Tea

Black tea is a type of tea that is fully oxidized, resulting in a rich, robust flavor and a deep, amber-colored brew. It is one of the most common types of tea, enjoyed all over the world for its bold taste and energizing effects.

The origins of black tea can be traced back to the ancient tea-growing regions of China, where it was known as "red tea" due to the color of the brewed tea. Black tea was introduced to the western world in the 17th century, where it quickly gained popularity and became a staple beverage in many countries.

To produce black tea, tea leaves are harvested from the Camellia sinensis plant and allowed to wither, removing moisture from the leaves and making them pliable. The leaves are then rolled or crushed to release their natural oils and enzymes, which react with the oxygen in the air to produce the characteristic black tea flavor. The flavor of black tea can vary greatly depending on the region it is grown in and the specific tea plant varietal used. Generally, black tea has a strong, bold flavor with notes of fruit, flowers, and spices and a slightly astringent finish. It is typically enjoyed with milk and sugar, which helps to balance out its bold flavor.

Black tea is rich in antioxidants, which help protect the body from the damaging effects of free radicals. These antioxidants have been linked to various health benefits, including a reduced risk of heart disease, cancer, and cognitive decline.

Black tea is also known for its energizing effects. It contains caffeine, which is a natural stimulant that can help to improve focus and concentration, as well as boost physical performance. Unlike coffee, which can sometimes cause jitters and anxiety, black tea provides a more balanced, sustained energy boost.

Some of the most popular varieties of black tea include Darjeeling, Ceylon, and Assam. Darjeeling tea, which is grown in the Himalayan region of India, is known for its delicate, floral flavor, while Ceylon tea, grown in the highlands of Sri Lanka, has a bold, full-bodied flavor. Assam tea, which is grown in the Assam region of India, is known for its rich, malty flavor. In addition to these traditional black tea varieties, many flavored black teas are available, which are made by blending black tea with herbs, fruits, and spices. Some popular flavored black teas include Earl Grey, black tea blended with bergamot oil, and Chai, black tea blended with spices like cinnamon, cardamom, and ginger.

Whether enjoyed on its own or blended with other ingredients, black tea is a tasty and enjoyable way to start the day or provide a mid-afternoon pick-me-up.

Choosing the best Black Tea

Darjeeling

This tea is grown in the Darjeeling region of India and is known for its delicate, floral flavor and aroma. It is typically light in color and has a slightly astringent taste. Darjeeling is often referred to as the "Champagne of Teas" due to its refined and complex flavor profile.

Assam

This tea is grown in the Assam region of India and is known for its strong, full-bodied flavor and malty aroma. It is typically a deep, reddish-brown color and has a bold, robust taste. Assam is often used as the base for many blends, including breakfast teas and chai.

Keemun

This Chinese black tea is known for its complex, smoky flavor and sweet aroma. It is made from the small-leaved Chinese varietal of the tea plant and is grown in the Anhui province of China. Keemun tea is often used in blends due to its unique flavor profile.

Ceylon

Ceylon tea comes from Sri Lanka and is known for its bright, crisp flavor and golden-yellow color. It has a slightly sweet and slightly citrusy taste and is often used in blends with other teas or fruits. Ceylon is also a popular choice for iced tea due to its refreshing flavor.

Yunnan

This Chinese black tea is famous for its smooth, rich flavor and sweet aroma. It is made from the large-leaved Assam varietal of the tea plant and is grown in the Yunnan province of China. Yunnan tea is often considered a high-quality tea due to the care and attention that goes into its production.

Lapsang Souchong

This Chinese black tea has a distinctive smoky flavor, achieved by drying the tea leaves over a pine fire. It is made from the small-leaved Chinese varietal of the tea plant and is grown in the Fujian province of China. Lapsang Souchong tea is often considered an acquired taste due to its strong, smoky flavor.

Irish Breakfast

Irish breakfast tea is a robust blend of black teas that are typically made with Assam, Kenyan, and Ceylon teas. It is known for its strong, full-bodied flavor and bold, malty taste. Irish breakfast tea is often served with milk and sugar and is a popular choice for a hearty morning pick-me-up.

Nilgiri

This Indian black tea has a light, floral flavor and bright, golden color when brewed. It is made from the small-leaved Chinese varietal of the tea plant and is grown in the Nilgiri Hills of Southern India. Nilgiri tea is also known for its refreshing and invigorating qualities.

Earl Grey

Earl Grey tea is a type of black tea flavored with the oil of the bergamot orange, a small citrus fruit native to Italy. It is named after Charles Grey, the 2nd Earl Grey and British

Prime Minister in the 1830s. Earl Grey tea has a unique, citrusy aroma and a light, refreshing flavor.

English Breakfast

English breakfast tea is another popular blend of black teas that are often made with Assam, Kenyan, and Ceylon teas. It is known for its strong, full-bodied flavor and robust, slightly bitter taste. English breakfast tea is typically served with milk and is a popular choice for a hearty morning meal.

Green Tea

Green tea is a type of tea that is made from the leaves of the Camellia sinensis plant. It is a popular drink in many parts of the world and is known for its many health benefits.

The origins of green tea can be traced back to China, where it has been consumed for thousands of years. It was first used as a medicinal drink and was believed to have many healing properties. In recent years, green tea has gained popularity in Western countries and is now widely available in many different forms.

There are several key differences between green tea and other types of tea. Unlike black and oolong teas, green tea leaves are not fermented, retaining many of their natural compounds and nutrients. This gives green tea its unique taste and health benefits.

One of the key compounds in green tea is catechins, which are a type of antioxidant. These compounds help to protect the body from free radicals, which are harmful molecules that can cause damage to cells and tissues. Green tea also contains a small amount of caffeine, which can help to improve focus and concentration.

One of the most well-known benefits of green tea is its ability to help with weight loss. Green tea contains a compound called EGCG, which has been shown to boost metabolism and help the body burn fat more efficiently. Green tea is also good for the heart. It has been shown to help lower cholesterol levels and reduce the risk of heart disease. It can also help reduce inflammation in the body, which is linked to several chronic conditions. Last but not least, green tea contains no calories and is low in caffeine, which makes it a great alternative to sugary drinks and caffeine-laden beverages. It can also help to improve digestion and regulate blood sugar levels.

There are many different ways to enjoy green tea. It can be consumed hot or cold and is available in a variety of flavors. Some people like to drink it plain, while others prefer to add honey or lemon for a touch of sweetness. Green tea can also be used in cooking and is a common ingredient in many Asian dishes.

Choosing the best Green tea

Gyokuro

This high-quality, shade-grown Japanese green tea is recognized for its delicate flavor and bright green color. It is made from young tea leaves that are grown in the shade for about 20 days before harvest, which helps to increase the levels of chlorophyll and amino acids in the leaves. This results in a tea with a smooth, sweet taste and a slightly vegetal flavor.

Matcha

This is a finely ground powder made from green tea leaves that are grown in the shade and then ground into a fine powder. It is traditionally used in Japanese tea ceremonies and is known for its bright green color and bold, earthy flavor. Matcha is a rich source of antioxidants and has been shown to have many potential health benefits.

Dragonwell

This green tea from China has flat, spear-shaped leaves and a delicate, nutty flavor to it. It is made from young tea leaves that are harvested in the spring and then pan-fried to preserve their delicate flavor and aroma. Dragonwell is often considered one of the best green teas in China and is highly prized for its unique flavor and appearance.

Gunpowder

This Chinese green tea is distinguished by its tightly curled leaves, which resemble gunpowder pellets. It has a robust, grassy flavor and a bold, full-bodied flavor. Gunpowder tea is made from young tea leaves that are rapidly rolled and dried to retain flavor and aroma.

Sencha

Noted for its bright green color and delicate, grassy flavor, this popular Japanese green tea is made from young tea leaves that have been steamed, rolled, and dried to preserve their flavor and aroma. Sencha is often served as a daily tea in Japan and is enjoyed for its refreshing flavor and natural sweetness.

Bancha

This type of green tea from Japan is made from older tea leaves that are harvested later in the season. It has a mild, slightly astringent flavor and is known for its coarser, more rustic appearance. Bancha is often used as a daily tea in Japan and is appreciated for its lower caffeine content and affordable price.

Hojicha

Hojicha is a Japanese green tea produced from roasted tea leaves with a distinct toasty flavor and a reddish brown hue. It has a moderate, slightly nutty flavor and is noted for having a reduced caffeine level, making it an excellent choice for caffeine-sensitive people or those seeking a soothing evening tea.

White Tea

White tea is recognized for its delicate and refined flavor. It is made from the tea plant's unopened buds and young leaves, harvested when they are still covered in fine white downy hair. The tea is then carefully processed to retain as much of the natural goodness and flavor as possible, resulting in a light and fragrant tea that is perfect for those who prefer a more subtle and refined taste.

The name "white tea" comes from the delicate white hairs covering the young tea leaves and buds when harvested. These hairs give the tea its distinctive light and silvery appearance, which is why it is known as "white" tea.

White tea is primarily grown in the Fujian province of China, which has a climate ideal for tea cultivation. The high humidity and warm temperatures in this region help to create the perfect conditions for the tea plants to thrive, producing leaves that are rich in flavor and aroma. In addition to China, white tea is also grown in other regions around the world, including India, Sri Lanka, and Taiwan. Each of these regions has its own unique growing conditions and terroir, which results in a range of different white tea flavors and aromas.

One of the key benefits of white tea is its low oxidation level, which is achieved by minimizing the amount of handling and processing the tea leaves undergo. This results in a tea that is rich in antioxidants and nutrients, making it an excellent choice for those looking to improve their health and well-being.

To preserve the freshness of white tea, it should be brewed at a relatively low temperature using clean, pure water that is not quite boiling, around 175 to 190 degrees Fahrenheit. Water boils at 212 degrees Fahrenheit, so the water should be hot but not simmer. The length of time that the tea should steep will depend on the variety, but it can be anywhere from one minute to five minutes. A teaspoon of leaves per eight-ounce cup may be sufficient if the tea is made up of compact buds. If the leaves are open and light, you may need closer to a tablespoon per cup. It is best to taste the tea before adding any sweeteners or other ingredients, as white tea may not need them.

Despite its name, white tea is not necessarily white when brewed. Depending on the type of tea and the brewing conditions, the brewed tea can range in color from pale yellow to amber.

Choosing the best White tea

Silver Needle

This white tea, recognized for its delicate flavor and silvery appearance, is prepared from only the best young buds of the tea plant. When brewed, Silver Needle has a pale yellow color and a subtle, sweet flavor with hints of grass and honey. It is grown in the Fujian province of China and is considered one of the highest-quality white teas.

White Peony

This white tea has a little stronger flavor than Silver Needle since it is prepared from a blend of young tea leaves and silver buds. It is also produced in China's Fujian province and is noted for its sweet and flowery overtones. White Peony has a pale yellow color and a delicate, floral aroma with undertones of sweet fruit when brewed.

Long Life Eyebrow

Long Life Eyebrow white tea is a high-quality, delicately flavored tea named after the shape of the leaves, which resemble long, thin eyebrows. It is characterized by its light yellow color and a slightly sweet and floral taste. It is low in caffeine, making it a perfect choice for those who are sensitive to caffeine or want a relaxing beverage. Long-Life Eyebrow is also known for its beauty benefits since it is believed to help improve the appearance of the skin and may help to reduce the appearance of fine lines and wrinkles.

Shoumei

This white tea is made from larger, more mature leaves of the tea plant and has a slightly more robust flavor than other white teas. When brewed, Shoumei has a pale yellow color and a smooth, mellow flavor with hints of sweetness and a hint of astringency. It is grown in the Fujian province of China and is known for its smooth, full-bodied taste.

Darjeeling White

This white tea is grown in the Darjeeling region of India and is made from the first flush of tea leaves, giving it a delicate and floral flavor. It is known for its light, golden color, and delicate aroma. When brewed, Darjeeling White has a light golden color and a delicate, floral aroma with hints of sweet fruit.

Yinzhen

This white tea is made from only the finest young buds of the tea plant and is grown in the Fujian province of China. It is noted for its sweet, floral flavor and bright, golden color. When brewed, Yinzhen has a bright golden color and a sweet, floral flavor with hints of honey and grass.

Pai Mu Tan

This white tea is cultivated in the Chinese region of Fujian and is crafted from only the best young buds of the tea plant. It is distinguished by its delicate flavor and pale, light color. Pai Mu Tan has a pale yellow color and a delicate, floral aroma with hints of sweet fruits when brewed.

Hao Ya A

This white tea comes from China's Fujian province. It is made from a mix of young tea leaves and silver buds. It is known for its strong, full-bodied flavor and its golden color. When brewed, Hao Ya A has a bright golden color and a strong, full-bodied flavor with hints of sweetness and a hint of astringency.

Oolong Tea

Oolong tea is often overlooked in favor of the more well-known green and black teas. However, it has a unique flavor and health benefits that make it worth exploring.

This tea gets its name from the Chinese word "wu long," which means "black dragon." It is believed that the name originated from the dark, twisted leaves of some oolong teas, which resemble the scales of a dragon.

Oolong tea is primarily grown in China and Taiwan, although it is also produced in smaller quantities in other countries such as India and Thailand. In China, the main growing regions for oolong tea are the Fujian and Guangdong provinces, which are known for their misty, humid climates that are ideal for tea cultivation. Taiwan is also a major producer of oolong tea, with the mountainous regions of Nantou and Hsinchu being the primary growing areas.

Oolong tea plants are grown at high elevations and require a specific combination of sun, shade, and humidity to thrive. It is produced through a process that combines elements of both green and black tea production. The leaves are partially fermented, giving them a flavor that is between the grassy, vegetal notes of green tea and the malty, bold flavor of black tea. The level of oxidation and fermentation varies depending on the type of oolong tea being produced, resulting in a wide range of flavors and aromas. Because of this diversity in processing, Oolong tea is well-known for its complex, layered flavors, which can range from fruity to floral to nutty, depending on the variety.

Brewing oolong tea is a bit different than brewing other types of tea. The first step is to choose the right oolong tea for your taste preferences. Many types of oolong tea are available, ranging from light, floral teas to bold, dark teas. Once you have chosen your tea, the next step is to measure out the right amount. Oolong tea is usually brewed with smaller amounts of leaves than other teas, so be sure to follow the recommended serving size on the package.

Next, heat up some water to the right temperature for your tea. Let the water cool slightly before pouring it over the tea leaves to allow the flavors to develop fully. Oolong tea is usually brewed at a lower temperature than black tea, around 185-205 degrees Fahrenheit.

Steep the tea for the recommended amount of time, ranging from 3-5 minutes for lighter oolongs to 5-7 minutes for darker teas. Be sure to keep an eye on the clock, as over-steeping can produce a bitter, astringent flavor.

When the tea is made steeping, pour it into a cup and enjoy. Oolong tea can be re-steeped multiple times, so feel free to add more hot water to the leaves and steep again for a second or third cup.

In addition to its unique flavor, oolong tea also has several health benefits. It is high in antioxidants, which can help to protect against free radicals and promote overall health. It is also believed to have metabolism-boosting properties, making it a popular choice for those looking to lose weight.

Choosing the best Oolong tea

Tie Guan Yin

Often referred to as the "Iron Goddess of Mercy," Tie Guan Yin is one of China's most popular oolong teas. Tie oolong tea is grown in the Fujian province of China and is known for its smooth, creamy flavor and floral aroma.

Dong Ding

Also called "Frozen Summit," this oolong tea from Taiwan's Nantou County is famous for its roasted, nutty flavor and rich, amber hue. This type of tea grows at high altitudes.

Phoenix Dancong

This oolong tea from China's Guangdong province is famous for its unique flavor profile, which includes notes of honey, fruit, and florals. It is also referred to as "Phoenix Single Shrub" because it is made from the leaves of a single bush.

THE TEA LOVER'S BIBLE

Wuyi Yan Cha

This oolong tea from China's Wuyi Mountains is recognized for its robust, smokey flavor and dark, amber hue. It is also known as "Rock Tea" since it is produced on rocky cliffs in the mountains.

Ali Shan

Noted for its delicate, floral flavor and light green color, this tea is often referred to as "Ali Mountain" for it is grown on the slopes of the Alishan mountains in the Alishan region of Taiwan.

Anxi Tie Guan Yin

This oolong tea is grown in the Anxi County of China. It is often referred to as "Tie Guan Yin from Anxi" due to the fact that it is grown in the same region as Tie Guan Yin but has a slightly different flavor profile. This tea has a smooth, floral flavor and golden color.

High Mountain Oolong

Grown at high altitudes in Taiwan, this tea is known for its light, floral flavor and pale green color. It is also called "Gao Shan Oolong" since it is grown on the high mountain slopes of Taiwan.

Pu-erh Tea

Also known as aged or fermented tea, pu-erh tea has been enjoyed for centuries in China. It is now gaining popularity in the Western world for its unique taste and potential health benefits.

Pu-erh tea comes from the Camellia sinensis plant, the same plant that produces black, green, and white teas. The difference lies in the processing method, which involves a unique fermentation process. The leaves are picked, withered, rolled, and then allowed to ferment before being dried and aged. This process can take anywhere from a few months to several years, resulting in a tea with a deep, rich flavor and a dark reddish-brown color.

One of the most notable characteristics of pu-erh tea is its ability to improve with age. As the tea is aged, the flavors become more complex, and the tea becomes smoother and less bitter. This has made pu-erh tea a popular choice for collectors and connoisseurs, with some teas being aged for decades and fetching high prices.

Pu-erh tea is also often enjoyed as a tea cake or brick, where the tea leaves are compressed into a specific shape and then aged. These tea cakes can be stored and aged for several years, with the flavor and value of the tea increasing over time.

Pu-erh tea is known for its high caffeine content, making it a popular choice for those looking for a caffeine boost. The caffeine consistency of pu-erh tea varies depending on factors such as the age and fermentation process of the tea leaves. Younger, raw pu-erh tea tends to have a higher caffeine content compared to aged, fermented pu-erh tea. This is because the caffeine in the tea leaves breaks down over time during the fermentation process, resulting in a lower caffeine content. The brewing method also plays a role in the caffeine consistency of pu-erh tea. Using a shorter steeping time or using cooler water will result in a lower caffeine concentration while using a longer steeping time or hotter water will result in a higher caffeine concentration.

Choosing the best Pu-ehr tea

<u>Da Zhong Pu-Erh Tea</u>

Produced in the Yunnan province of China, it is known for its strong, bold flavor. This tea is traditionally aged for several years before being sold, which adds depth and complexity to its taste.

<u>Ripe Pu-Erh Tea</u>

Ripe Pu-Erh tea is made from fully fermented tea leaves and has a smooth, mellow flavor. It is often aged for several years before being sold, giving it a rich, earthy taste.

<u>Aged Raw Pu-Erh Tea</u>

This type of pu-erh tea is made from unfermented tea leaves that are aged for several years before being sold. It has a more delicate, floral flavor compared to ripe pu erh tea and is often considered more refined and refined.

<u>Organic Pu-Erh Tea</u>

This tea is produced using organic farming methods, which means it is free from synthetic chemicals and pesticides. It has a more pure, natural flavor and is often considered healthier than non-organic pu-erh tea.

Other Teas

<u>Purple Tea</u>

Purple tea is a relatively new and unique variety of tea that hails from the high-altitude regions of Kenya. It has recently gained popularity due to its health benefits and distinct flavor.

Purple tea comes from the same plant species used to produce all other types of tea. However, it is unique because it contains high levels of anthocyanins, a type of flavonoid pigment that gives the leaves their distinctive purple color. These anthocyanins are also found in other purple-hued fruits and vegetables like blueberries, grapes, and purple potatoes.

The tea is grown at high altitudes of around 6,500-7,000 feet above sea level in the fertile soil of the Kenyan Rift Valley. The high altitude and cool climate, and rich soil create the perfect conditions for the tea to thrive and develop its unique flavor and nutritional properties.

The tea leaves are harvested by hand, carefully plucked from the plant, and then processed using traditional methods. The leaves are withered, rolled, oxidized, and dried to produce the final product. The resulting tea is a vibrant purple color with a delicate, floral aroma and a slightly sweet, fruity flavor.

Purple tea is known for its numerous health benefits. Its high levels of anthocyanins make it a potent antioxidant, helping to protect the body from the damaging effects of free radicals and other toxins. These anthocyanins are also thought to have anti-inflammatory properties, making the tea beneficial for conditions like arthritis and other inflammatory diseases.

The tea also contains other beneficial compounds like catechins and polyphenols, which are known to positively affect heart health. Regular consumption of purple tea has been shown to reduce the risk of heart disease and stroke, as well as to lower blood pressure and improve cholesterol levels.

When it comes to the flavor profile, purple tea has a slightly sweet, fruity taste with a delicate floral aroma, making it a refreshing and enjoyable beverage. It can be enjoyed hot or iced and blended with other ingredients to create unique and flavorful blends.

Rooibos Tea

Rooibos tea is a type of herbal tea made from the leaves of the Aspalathus linearis plant, which is native to South Africa. It is sometimes referred to as "red tea" because of the reddish color of the brewed beverage.

It can be enjoyed on its own or combined with other herbs and spices to create a variety of flavored teas. It can also be used as an ingredient in different recipes, such as baked goods and cocktails.

<u>What makes it different from other teas?</u>

- Caffeine – Rooibos tea is naturally caffeine-free. Traditional teas, on the other hand, contain caffeine, which can have a stimulating effect on the body. Rooibos tea is a good choice for people who are sensitive to caffeine or who want to avoid it for other reasons.

- Tannin – Rooibos tea has a lower tannin content compared to traditional teas. Tannins are compounds that can give the tea a slightly bitter taste and can also interfere with the absorption of certain nutrients in the body. Rooibos tea has a naturally sweet and slightly nutty flavor, and its low tannin content makes it less likely to taste bitter.

- Health benefits - Rooibos tea is high in antioxidants, which can help to protect the body from damage caused by free radicals. It is also rich in minerals such as iron, calcium, and zinc, which can support a healthy immune system. Traditional teas also have some health benefits, but they may not be as high in antioxidants or minerals as rooibos tea.

Yellow Tea

Yellow tea is a type of tea that is less well-known than other varieties. It is primarily produced in China and is characterized by a yellow-hued liquor when brewed.

The production process for yellow tea is similar to that of green tea but with an additional step of slow, controlled oxidation. This step gives yellow tea its unique flavor profile, which is often described as mellower and less astringent than green tea.

Yellow tea is typically harvested in the spring, and the leaves are carefully hand-picked to ensure that only the highest quality ones are used. The leaves are then pan-fired to halt the oxidation process and then left to rest in a controlled environment until they turn yellow. The final step is to dry the leaves to preserve their flavor and aroma.

This tea is a rare and precious commodity, as it is not produced in large quantities. It is typically more expensive than other types of tea, but it is well worth the price for those who appreciate its unique flavor and health benefits.

Herbal teas

Unlike regular teas, made from the Camellia sinensis leaves, herbal infusions - also known as herbal teas – are made from various herbs, flowers, and other plant materials. These infusions have been used for centuries to support many health conditions and are a great addition to any wellness routine.

Herbal infusions are made by steeping herbs in hot water to extract active compounds and essential oils. The resulting liquid is then consumed as tea, providing a convenient and tasty way to enjoy the benefits of herbs. Some popular herbs for infusions include chamomile, peppermint, ginger, and lavender, each with its own unique health benefits.

One of the main advantages of herbal infusions is their ability to support the body's natural healing processes. Many herbs have antioxidant, anti-inflammatory, and immune-boosting properties, which can help to reduce the risk of chronic diseases and promote overall health. For example, chamomile is known for its calming and sleep-promoting effects, while ginger is often used to alleviate nausea and digestive issues.

While herbal infusions are generally considered safe, it's essential to use them wisely and consult a healthcare provider before incorporating them into your routine. Some herbs may interact with medications or have side effects, so it's important to do your research and choose the right herbs for your needs.

CHAPTER FIVE

How to Make the Perfect Cup of Tea

There is nothing quite like a perfectly brewed cup of tea. Whether you prefer black tea, green tea, herbal tea, or a blend of your own creation, the key to a perfect cup of tea lies in the preparation. With a bit of care and attention to detail, you can enjoy a delicious and satisfying cup of tea every time.

The first essential step in preparing a perfect tea cup is choosing the right tea. Select a high-quality tea that is fresh and fragrant. Avoid teas that are old or have been sitting on the shelf for an extended time, as they will not have the same flavor and aroma as fresh tea.

Once you have selected your tea, the next step is to measure the right amount. The general rule of thumb is to use one teaspoon of tea leaves per cup of water. However, this can vary depending on the type of tea and your personal preference. Experiment with different amounts to find the perfect balance for your taste.

Next, heat the water to the proper temperature. Different teas require different water temperatures for optimal flavor. For black and herbal teas, bring the water to a full boil. Heat the water to about 175-180 degrees Fahrenheit for green tea and 150-160 degrees Fahrenheit for white tea.

Once the water is heated, it's time to steep the tea. Place the tea leaves in a tea strainer or tea ball and let them steep in hot water for the recommended amount of time. The steeping time can vary depending on the type of tea, so be sure to follow the instructions on the packaging. Oversteeping can result in a bitter flavor, so be sure to keep an eye on the time.

Prepare the cups or teapot while the tea is steeping. If you're using cups, prepare them by washing them with hot water to keep the tea warm while you drink it. If you're using a teapot, preheat it by pouring a small amount of hot water into the pot. This will keep the tea hot as it steeps.

Once the tea has finished steeping, remove the tea leaves from the water and pour the tea into the cups or the teapot. If you're using a teapot, be sure to pour the tea through a strainer to catch any loose leaves. Serve the tea immediately, as it will begin to cool quickly.

For the perfect cup of tea, add the right amount of milk or sweetener, if desired. Some teas, such as black tea, are traditionally served with milk, while others, such as green tea, are best enjoyed without. Experiment with different combinations to find the perfect balance for your taste.

In addition to these essential steps, a few other factors can help you prepare a perfect cup of tea. For example, using high-quality water will help bring out the flavor of the tea.

Avoid using tap water that is heavily chlorinated or has a strong mineral taste, as this can affect the flavor of the tea. Instead, use filtered or spring water for the best results.

Another factor to consider is the quality of your tea accessories. Investing in good-quality tea accessories will help you brew the perfect cup of tea every time. Using a high-quality tea strainer or tea ball will help prevent loose leaves from ending up in your cup, while a good-quality teapot will help keep your tea warm as you enjoy it.

The Art of Brewing Tea

Brewing tea is a delicate art that requires patience and attention to detail. With a wide variety of teas available, each with its unique flavor profile, it's no surprise that there are many different ways to brew the perfect cup.

Traditional tea brewing techniques

The Chinese Gong Fu method of tea brewing originated in the Fujian province of China. This method involves using a small teapot, called a gaiwan, and a small teacup, called a cha hai. The gaiwan is used to steep the tea, and the cha hai is used to hold the brewed tea until it is ready to be poured into individual cups.

To brew tea using the Gong Fu method, the tea leaves must be placed in the gaiwan, and hot water must be added. The tea is steeped for a short time, usually just a few seconds, before being poured into the cha hai. The tea is then poured into individual cups and enjoyed.

One of the benefits of the Gong Fu method is that it allows the tea drinker to control the strength and flavor of the tea. By adjusting the number of tea leaves and the steeping time, the tea can be brewed to the desired strength. This method also allows the tea drinker to experience the full range of flavors in the tea, as the short steeping times preserve the delicate aromas and flavors.

The Japanese Tea Ceremony, also known as the Way of Tea, is a centuries-old ritual involving preparing and drinking matcha, a powdered green tea. The ceremony is steeped in tradition and symbolism, and every aspect of the ritual is carefully planned and executed.

The ceremony host carefully measures the matcha powder to prepare the tea and sifts it into a bowl. Hot water is added to the bowl, and the tea is whisked using a bamboo whisk called a chasen. The whisking motion is important, as it creates a frothy texture in the tea and helps to evenly distribute the matcha powder.

The Japanese Tea Ceremony is a meditative and peaceful experience, focusing on mindfulness and enjoying the present moment. Once the tea is prepared, it is poured into small cups and served to the guests. The guests then take turns drinking the tea and appreciating its flavor and aroma.

In addition to these methods, there are many other traditional tea brewing techniques from around the world. For example, in India, tea is often brewed using a metal pot called a chaiwallah, and in Turkey, tea is brewed in a special double-walled glass called a cezve.

Modern Tea Brewing Techniques

Tea brewing techniques have come a long way since the days of simply boiling water and steeping a tea bag. Today, there are many ways to brew tea, each with its unique characteristics and flavors.

Kettle or teapot

To brew tea using a kettle or teapot, bring water to the desired temperature (usually between 160 and 180 degrees Fahrenheit for most teas) and pour it over the tea leaves in the pot. Allow the tea to steep for the recommended time (usually between 3 and 5 minutes for most teas), then strain the tea into cups and enjoy. This method allows for control over the temperature and steeping time of the tea and the ability to see the tea as it steeps.

Tea infuser

A tea infuser is a small, perforated container that holds the tea leaves and can be easily removed from the water once the tea has reached the desired strength. To brew tea using a tea infuser, simply place the tea leaves in the infuser and steep them in hot water for the recommended time. Once the tea has reached the desired strength, remove the infuser and enjoy.

Cold brewing is the next technique, which involves steeping tea in cold water for an extended period, usually 8-12 hours. This method results in a smoother, less bitter flavor compared to hot brewing and is often used for iced tea. To cold brew tea, place the tea leaves in a pitcher or jar of cold water and let steep in the refrigerator for 8-12 hours. Once the tea has reached the desired strength, strain the tea and enjoy over ice.

French Press

Have you ever heard of the French press? A French press is a coffee maker that can also be used to brew tea. To use a French press for tea, put the tea leaves in the press, pour in hot water, and let steep for the recommended time. Once the tea has reached the desired strength, press the plunger down to separate the tea leaves from the liquid and pour into cups to enjoy.

Each modern tea brewing technique has unique benefits and flavor characteristics. Cold brewing results in a smoother, less bitter flavor, and using a French press allows for a full-bodied, rich cup of tea. Using a tea kettle or teapot allows for precise control over the brewing process, while a tea infuser makes it easy to remove the tea leaves once the tea has reached the desired strength. No matter which method you choose, experimenting with different tea brewing techniques can help you discover new flavors and find your perfect cup of tea.

Finding the Ideal Water Temperature and Steeping Time

About Water Temperature

When it comes to brewing tea, the temperature of the water plays a crucial role in the flavor and quality of the tea. Different types of tea require different temperatures to extract the maximum flavor and aroma. For example, green tea should be brewed at a lower temperature than black tea, as it tends to become bitter and astringent if it is brewed at a higher temperature.

The ideal temperature for brewing tea depends on the type of tea being used. Water that is too hot can burn the leaves and destroy the delicate flavors and aromas of the tea. On the other hand, water that is too cold can result in a weak and flavorless cup of tea.

Green tea is known for its delicate flavors and aromas and is best brewed at a temperature of around 80-85°C. The lower temperature helps to preserve the delicate flavors and aromas of the tea, and it also helps to prevent the tea from becoming bitter and astringent.

On the other hand, black tea should be brewed at a higher temperature of around 90-95°C. The higher temperature helps extract the tea's full flavor and aroma, and it also helps prevent the tea from becoming weak and flavorless.

Oolong tea is a type of tea that falls between green and black tea in terms of flavor and aroma. It is best brewed at a temperature of around 85-90°C to extract the full flavor and aroma of the tea without burning the leaves.

Herbal teas, such as chamomile and peppermint, should be brewed at a lower temperature of around 70-80°C. The lower temperature helps to preserve the delicate flavors and aromas of the herbs, and it also helps to prevent the tea from becoming bitter and astringent.

In addition to the type of tea, the temperature of the water can also be affected by factors such as the quality of the water, the altitude, and the type of teapot or kettle being used. For example, water that is high in minerals can affect the flavor and aroma of the tea, and it can also affect the temperature at which the tea is brewed.

Altitude can also affect the temperature of the water, as the water boils at a lower temperature at higher altitudes. This means that tea brewed at high altitudes will require a lower brewing temperature than tea brewed at lower altitudes.

The type of tea pot or kettle used can also affect the temperature of the water. For example, a kettle with a temperature control feature can help to maintain the ideal brewing temperature for different types of tea.

About Steeping Time

Infusion time, also known as steeping time, is when tea leaves are left to steep in hot water before being removed and consumed. It is an essential factor in the tea-making process as it can significantly affect the taste and aroma of the final brew.

Different tea varieties require varying infusion times to extract the optimal flavor and aroma from the tea leaves. When it comes to tea making, the infusion time is largely dependent on the type of tea being brewed. For example, black tea leaves typically require a longer infusion time than green tea leaves, as black tea leaves generally are larger and denser.

The infusion time can also be influenced by personal preference and individual taste. Some tea enthusiasts may prefer a stronger, bolder flavor and therefore opt for a longer infusion time. Others may prefer a more subtle and delicate flavor and may choose a shorter infusion time.

Generally, the ideal infusion time for most tea varieties is between 3 and 5 minutes. This allows for the tea leaves to release their flavor and aroma into the hot water without becoming oversteeped, which can result in a bitter and unpleasant taste.

Remember that tea leaves continue to release their flavor and aroma even after the infusion time has ended. This means that leaving the tea leaves in hot water for longer than the recommended infusion time can result in an over-steeped brew, which can be unpleasant and bitter.

To prevent oversteeping, removing the tea leaves from the hot water is recommended once the desired infusion time has been reached. This can be done using a tea infuser or strainer or simply by pouring the tea into a separate cup or pot.

How to Choose Your Tea Equipment

Tea Kettle

Choosing a tea kettle can be a daunting task, especially with the many available options. Not only do you have to consider the design and aesthetics of the kettle, but also its functionality and durability. Here are some key factors to consider when choosing your tea kettle.

Material

The material of the tea kettle is an important factor to consider as it determines the durability and performance of the kettle. The most common materials used for tea kettles are stainless steel, copper, and cast iron.

Stainless steel is the most popular choice for tea kettles as it is durable, rust-resistant, and easy to clean. Cast iron tea kettles are heavy and sturdy, but they take longer to heat up and require more care and cleaning to avoid rusting. Copper is a great option as it is an excellent heat conductor, but it requires more maintenance and can be quite expensive.

Capacity

Before choosing a tea kettle, consider the size of your household and how much tea you typically make. If you are a solo tea drinker, a small kettle with a 1-2 cups capacity will suffice. However, if you often have guests over or have a large family, opt for a kettle with a higher capacity of 4-6 cups. This will ensure that you have enough hot water for everyone, and you won't have to constantly refill the kettle.

Heat source

Tea kettles can be heated on a stovetop or via electricity. Stovetop kettles are heated on a gas or electric burner and come in a variety of materials, including stainless steel, copper, and cast iron. Electric kettles are more convenient as they have an automatic shut-off feature and can be plugged into any outlet. However, they can be less durable and may not be as efficient in heating water as stovetop kettles.

Design and aesthetics

When choosing a tea kettle, consider the design and aesthetics that will complement your kitchen. Tea kettles come in a range of styles, from traditional to modern, so you can choose the one that fits your personal style and kitchen décor.

Additional features

Some tea kettles come with additional features such as a whistling mechanism, a stay-cool handle, or a built-in infuser. A whistling kettle will alert you when the water is ready, while a stay-cool handle will prevent you from burning your hand when pouring the hot water. A built-in infuser is a great feature for loose-leaf tea lovers as it allows you to steep your tea directly in the kettle.

Take the time to research, compare different options, and choose the kettle that best fits your needs and preferences. A good tea kettle not only enhances the tea-making experience but also adds a touch of elegance to your kitchen.

Tea Strainer

When it comes to enjoying a cup of tea, choosing the right tea strainer can make all the difference. Not only does a good strainer help to infuse the tea leaves correctly, but it also helps to keep any stray leaves out of your cup. With so many different options on the market, it can be overwhelming to choose the right one. Here are some key factors to consider when selecting a tea strainer.

Material

Some common options include stainless steel, silicone, and ceramic. Stainless steel strainers are durable and easy to clean but can be prone to rust. Silicone strainers are flexible and non-stick, making them great for loose-leaf tea, but they may not hold up well over time. Ceramic strainers are attractive and can be heated to keep your tea warm, but they are more fragile and can be difficult to clean.

Size

If you are using a small tea cup or mug, you will want to choose a smaller strainer that fits easily into the cup. On the other hand, a larger strainer may be necessary if you use a larger teapot or infuser. Be sure to measure the opening of your cup or teapot before choosing a strainer to ensure it will fit properly.

Shape

The shape of the strainer is also an essential factor to consider. Some common shapes include circular, oval, and rectangular. Circular strainers are the most common and fit easily into most cups and teapots. Oval strainers are great for fitting into wider cups or teapots, and rectangular strainers are great for straining larger amounts of tea at once.

Holes

A strainer with more holes will allow more water to flow through the tea leaves, resulting in a stronger infusion. On the other hand, a strainer with fewer holes will result in a weaker infusion. The size of the holes is also important, as larger holes may allow small tea leaves to escape into your cup.

Handle

A long handle allows for easy removal from the cup or teapot without burning your fingers. A handle with a hook or loop is also useful for hanging the strainer when not in use.

Additional Features

Some strainers come with additional features such as a lid or built-in infuser. A lid is useful for keeping the tea warm while it steeps, and a built-in infuser allows for easy removal of the tea leaves after steeping.

What do you like to drink your tea from?

The tea is ready and we have to decide which container to drink it from. From delicate teacups to sturdy mugs, the options are seemingly endless. But which one is the best for enjoying your favorite brew?

First, let's consider the classic teacup. These delicate vessels are often made of fine china or porcelain and feature intricate designs and patterns. They are perfect for formal occasions, such as afternoon tea or dinner parties. The small size of teacups also allows for precise control over the temperature of the tea, as the hot liquid will cool more quickly in a smaller container.

However, teacups can be fragile and may not be the best option for everyday use. They also don't offer much room for added ingredients like milk or honey. For a more practical option, consider using a mug. Mugs are generally made of sturdier materials, such as ceramic or porcelain, and come in different sizes and designs. They are perfect for enjoying tea on the go and offer plenty of room for added ingredients.

If you want to elevate your tea-drinking experience even further, consider using a glass teapot or infuser. These containers allow for a more visually appealing experience, as the tea can be watched as it steeps. They also allow for easy temperature control, as the tea can be seen cooling in the glass. However, be aware that glass is fragile and may not be the best option for everyday use.

A kyusu, or traditional Japanese teapot, is another option to consider. These teapots are typically made of ceramic and have a small handle and pouring spout for ease of use. They are ideal for brewing loose-leaf tea and allow for a more precise and controlled brewing process.

Whatever container you choose, make sure to clean and maintain it to get the finest tea-drinking experience possible. Regularly washing with warm water and mild soap will help keep your teapot, mug, or cup in top shape.

Additives to Make Your Tea Taste Better

Milk and Sugar

One of the most common debates among tea lovers is the addition of sugar and milk to tea. Some people swear by it, while others prefer plain and unsweetened tea. So what is the right way to make tea, and does adding sugar and milk really make a difference?

First, let's talk about the role of sugar in tea. Some people add sugar to their tea because it makes the drink sweeter and more enjoyable. This can be especially appealing if the tea is bitter or astringent. However, it's important to remember that sugar is a source of empty calories, and too much of it can contribute to weight gain and other health problems.

On the other hand, adding a small amount of sugar to tea can actually enhance the flavor of the tea itself. The sweetness can help balance out any bitterness or astringency and bring out the subtler flavors in the tea. In fact, many tea connoisseurs recommend adding a small amount of sugar to some types of tea, particularly black teas and oolong teas.

But what about milk? Is it really necessary to add milk to tea, or is it just a matter of personal preference?

For many people, adding milk to tea is an essential part of the tea-making process. Milk adds a rich, creamy flavor to the tea and can help smooth out any rough edges or bitterness. It also adds a different texture to the drink, which can be especially appealing if you want something more luxurious than plain water.

However, it's important to remember that milk is a source of fat and calories, so if you're trying to watch your weight or maintain a healthy lifestyle, you may want to limit the amount of milk you add to your tea. You can also try using low-fat or skim milk to reduce the caloric content of your tea, or you can experiment with different types of milk, such as almond milk or soy milk, which can add their own unique flavors to the drink.

Ultimately, deciding to add sugar and milk to your tea is personal. Some people love the added sweetness and creaminess, while others prefer plain and unsweetened tea. The important thing is to find a balance that works for you and to enjoy your tea however you like it best. So whether you're a traditionalist who prefers their tea with a splash of milk and a spoonful of sugar, or a purist who likes their tea plain and simple, remember that there's no right or wrong way to make tea – it's all about what you enjoy.

Add Some Spice to Your Tea

Adding spices to tea blends can bring a whole new level of flavor and warmth to your cup of tea. Whether you're a seasoned tea drinker or new to the world of tea, experimenting with spices can take your tea-drinking experience to the next level.

Many different spices can be added to tea blends, and your imagination limits the options. Common spices used in tea blends include cinnamon, cloves, ginger, cardamom, and nutmeg. These spices can be used alone or in combination to create unique and delicious flavors.

Cinnamon is a popular spice to add to tea blends because of its warm, sweet flavor. It pairs well with any kind of tea, including black, green, and herbal teas. Cinnamon can help to improve circulation and has been used for centuries as a natural remedy for colds and flu.

Cloves are another spice that is commonly added to tea blends. They have a strong, spicy flavor that is both warming and soothing. Cloves can be combined with other spices, such as cinnamon and ginger, to create a rich and flavorful tea blend.

Ginger is another spice that is commonly used in tea blends. It has a spicy, pungent flavor that is both warming and soothing. Ginger can help to improve digestion and has been used for centuries as a natural remedy for nausea and stomach upset.

Cardamom is a spice often used in tea blends because of its sweet, spicy flavor. It pairs well with both black and green teas and can help with digestion and bloating.

Nutmeg is a spice commonly added to tea blends because of its warm, sweet flavor. It pairs well with black, green, and herbal teas and can help to improve digestion and reduce bloating.

In addition to these common spices, many other herbs can be added to tea blends to create unique and delicious flavors. Some other spices to consider adding to your tea blends include allspice, anise, star anise, and fennel.

To create your own unique tea blend, start by choosing a base tea. Depending on your preferences, this can be a black tea, green tea, or herbal tea. Once you have selected your base tea, you can experiment with different spices to create a blend tailored to your tastes.

When adding spices to your tea blends, it's important to start with a small amount and gradually increase the amount until you achieve the desired flavor. It's also important to remember that different spices have different intensity levels, so you may need to adjust the amounts of each spice to achieve the perfect balance of flavors.

CHAPTER SIX
The Secrets to Pairing Tea and Food

When it comes to enjoying a delicious meal, many people often overlook the importance of pairing their food with the right tea. Tea, like wine, can enhance the flavors of specific meals and provide an unforgettable and pleasurable dining experience.

The goal of pairing tea with food is to find a balance and a fit that enriches both the dish's flavor and the tea. If you want to amaze your guests at your next dinner party or simply have some fun at home, here's a beginner's guide to combining tea with food.

Pairing Criteria

When it comes to pairing food and tea, there are a few key criteria to keep in mind in order to create the perfect combination.

First and foremost, consider the flavor profiles of both the food and the tea. Bold, spicy foods tend to pair well with bold, full-bodied teas, such as black teas or oolong teas. On the other hand, delicate, lightly flavored foods such as seafood or salads are best matched with delicate, light teas such as green teas or white teas.

Another important factor to consider is the level of bitterness in the tea. Bitterness can be desirable in some teas, but it can also be overwhelming if not balanced with the right food. To balance the bitterness, pair bitter teas with rich, fatty foods that can help to cut through the bitterness and create a smoother, more balanced flavor. For example, a strong black tea would pair well with a rich chocolate dessert or creamy cheese.

In addition to flavor, the texture is also important when pairing food and tea. For example, a smooth, silky tea like white tea would pair well with a smooth, creamy dish such as a risotto or a silky soup. On the other hand, a more robust tea such as black tea would pair well with a hearty, textured dish such as a stew or a hearty salad.

Next, we must not overlook the temperature of both food and tea in our evaluation. Cold teas are best paired with cold dishes, whereas hot teas are best matched with hot foods. A hot black tea, for example, would pair well with a warm, comforting dish like soup, whilst a cold green tea would be the perfect accompaniment to a refreshing summer salad.

Lastly, consider the overall mood and atmosphere of the meal when pairing food and tea. For example, a relaxing, contemplative meal would be best paired with a calming, meditative tea such as a green tea or a white tea, while a more lively, a social meal would be better suited to a bolder, more vibrant tea such as a black tea or an oolong tea.

Black Tea

Pairing food and black tea can be a delicious and satisfying experience, but it can also be a bit intimidating for those who are new to the art of tea pairing. However, with a bit of knowledge and practice, anyone can master the art of pairing black tea with food and enjoy the many flavor combinations that can be achieved.

First, it is important to understand the basic characteristics of black tea. Black tea is a fully oxidized tea, which gives it its characteristic bold and robust flavor. Black tea is often described as having notes of malt, honey, and sometimes even chocolate or spice. Because of its bold flavor, black tea is often paired with rich and hearty foods, such as roasted meats and savory dishes.

One of the key factors to consider when pairing black tea with food is the intensity of the flavors. If the food and tea flavors are too similar, they may clash and overwhelm the palate. On the other hand, if the flavors are too different, they may not complement each other, and the overall taste experience may be dull. To avoid these pitfalls, you must find a balance between the flavors of the tea and the food.

One practical example of pairing black tea with food is to pair it with savory dishes that have rich, bold flavors. For example, a strong black tea such as a Darjeeling or Assam would pair well with a roasted lamb or beef dish, as the bold flavors of the tea can cut through the richness of the meat and add depth to the overall flavor profile. Another example would be to pair black tea with a hearty stew or soup, such as a hearty beef or lamb stew. The bold flavors of black tea can add depth and complexity to the rich, savory flavors of the stew, creating a satisfying and satisfying meal.

Another case is the pairing of black tea with sweet and rich desserts. Black tea is often paired with desserts such as chocolate cake, cheesecake, or even fruit tarts. The bold flavors of black tea can cut through the richness of the desserts and add depth and complexity to the overall flavor profile. For example, a black tea with notes of chocolate or spice, such as a Darjeeling or Assam, would pair well with a rich chocolate cake or cheesecake. The bold flavors of the tea can complement the rich flavors of the dessert, creating a delicious and satisfying dessert experience.

Green Tea

Green tea has a delicate, slightly grassy flavor that bold or spicy dishes can easily overpower. However, when paired with the right food, it can bring out subtle flavors and create a delightful and balanced meal. Here are key factors to consider when pairing green tea with food:

The intensity of the tea itself - Different types of green tea can have varying levels of bitterness, astringency, and sweetness, so it's important to choose a food that will complement the specific green tea you're drinking. For example, a light, sweet green tea like Sencha would pair well with a dish with a similar sweetness level, such as grilled chicken with a citrus glaze or grilled salmon with a honey glaze. On the other hand, a bolder, more astringent green tea like Matcha would pair well with a dish that has a bit more intensity, such as a spicy stir-fry or a savory miso soup.

The temperature of the tea - Green tea is typically served at a lower temperature than black tea, so it's better to choose dishes that the tea's warmth won't overpower. For example, a cold green tea would pair well with a refreshing salad or sushi, while a warm green tea would pair well with a hearty soup or a savory stew.

The flavors and aromas of the food - Green tea has a delicate flavor and aroma that bold or spicy dishes can easily overpower, so it's important to choose foods that will complement the tea's flavors without overpowering them. For example, green tea pairs well with dishes with a similar sweetness level, such as grilled chicken with a citrus glaze or grilled salmon with a honey glaze. It also pairs well with dishes that have a bit of spice, such as a spicy stir-fry or a savory miso soup.

- Sushi - The delicate, slightly sweet flavor of green tea complements the flavors of sushi, especially when the sushi is made with fish or seafood. Green tea also pairs well with tempura, a Japanese dish made of battered fried vegetables or seafood. The light, crispy texture of tempura pairs well with the delicate flavor of green tea.

- Chicken - The soft, slightly grassy flavor of green tea complements the mild flavor of chicken, especially when the chicken is grilled or roasted. Green tea also pairs well with fish, such as salmon or tuna, which have a similar level of delicacy and sweetness.

- Green tea also pairs well with other dishes, such as salads, soups, and stews. For example, a light, refreshing green tea would pair well with a crisp, refreshing salad, while a bolder, more astringent green tea would pair well with a hearty soup or stew.

White Tea

White tea is a light and delicate tea renowned for its gentle flavors and refreshing qualities. It is made from the young leaves and buds of the Camellia sinensis plant and is minimally oxidized. White tea pairs well with a wide range of dishes due to its delicate nature.

When pairing white tea with food, it is important to consider the tea's flavor profile. White tea has a light, slightly sweet, and floral flavor, with hints of honey and stone fruits. It also has a smooth, creamy texture that is perfect for pairing with light, refreshing dishes.

Because white tea is a delicate tea, it is best to brew it at a lower temperature and for a shorter amount of time than other teas. This will help to preserve the tea's subtle flavors and prevent the tea from becoming bitter. When considering the serving temperature of the tea, white tea is best served slightly cool or at room temperature, as boiling water can overwhelm the delicate flavors of the tea. For example, a cup of white tea pairs well with a light and refreshing salad or a chilled seafood dish.

- One of the best foods to pair with white tea is seafood. The light and delicate flavors of white tea complement the subtle flavors of seafood, and the tea's smooth texture helps to balance the dish's texture. For example, a cup of white tea pairs well with a light and refreshing seafood salad, grilled shrimp, or scallops.

- Another food that pairs well with white tea is fresh fruits and vegetables. The light and refreshing flavors of white tea complement the sweetness and crispness of fresh fruits and vegetables, and the tea's smooth texture helps to balance the textures of the dish. For example, a cup of white tea pairs well with a fruit salad or lightly steamed vegetables such as asparagus or zucchini.

- White tea also pairs well with rich and creamy dishes, such as cheeses and dairy products. The light and delicate flavors of white tea help balance the dish's richness, and the tea's smooth texture complements the creamy texture of the food. For example, a cup of white tea pairs well with a creamy cheese plate or a rich and creamy dessert such as crème brulee.

Oolong Tea

Pairing food and oolong tea is a delicate and nuanced art that requires a bit of experimentation and understanding of both the food and the tea. Oolong tea, a type of semi-oxidized tea that falls between green and black tea, has a complex and versatile flavor profile that can be enhanced or balanced by the right food pairing.

First and foremost, it's essential to consider the flavor profile of the specific oolong tea you are using. Oolongs can range from light and floral to dark and roasted, and each will require different food pairings to bring out its best flavor.

- For light and floral oolongs, such as Tie Guan Yin or Oriental Beauty, try pairing them with delicate, lightly flavored dishes such as steamed fish or chicken or sweet desserts such as fruit tarts or cream puffs. These teas can also be enhanced by the flavors of fresh herbs and spices, so try pairing them with dishes that use herbs like basil or mint or spices like cardamom or star anise.

- For darker and more roasted oolongs, such as Dong Ding or Tie Luo Han, try pairing them with bolder and richer dishes, such as braised meats or savory stews. These teas can also stand up to the flavors of charcuterie and cured meats, so try pairing them with a charcuterie board or a platter of prosciutto and melon.

When pairing oolong tea with desserts, consider the sweetness level of the dish. Light and floral oolongs can be enhanced by slightly sweet desserts, while darker and roasted oolongs can balance the sweetness of richer desserts such as chocolate cake or tiramisu.

Oolongs can range from thin and light-bodied to full-bodied and rich, and the body of the tea will affect how it pairs with food.

- For light-bodied oolongs, pair them with light and delicate dishes such as sushi or tempura. These teas can also enhance the flavors of fresh vegetables and fruits, so try pairing them with dishes that use fresh ingredients, like salads or fruit platters.

- For full-bodied oolongs, try pairing them with heartier dishes such as roast chicken or grilled steak. These teas can also stand up to the flavors of bold spices and sauces, so try pairing them with dishes that use spices like cumin and chili peppers or seasonings like hoisin or oyster sauce.

When pairing oolong tea with alcohol, consider the flavor profile and body of the tea as well as the flavor profile and alcohol content of the beverage. Light and floral oolongs can pair well with light and refreshing cocktails or white wines, while darker and roasted oolongs can pair well with richer and more complex cocktails or red wines.

Pu-her Tea

Pairing food and pu-ehr tea can be a delightful and unique experience for the palate. This ancient tea, also known as aged or fermented tea, has a rich, earthy flavor and a unique aroma that can enhance the flavors of many dishes.

Pu-ehr tea has a bold, earthy flavor that can be enhanced by pairing it with similar dishes. For example, dishes with a rich, savory flavor, such as roasted meats, can be enhanced by pu-ehr tea. The tea can also be paired with smoky dishes, such as grilled vegetables or smoked fish.

Another aspect to consider when pairing pu-ehr tea and food is the aroma of the tea. Pu-ehr tea has a distinctive earthy aroma that can be enhanced by pairing it with dishes with similar aromas. For example, dishes that have an herbal or earthy aroma, such as mushrooms or truffles, can be enhanced by pu-ehr tea. The tea can also be paired with dishes that have a spicy aroma, such as curries or spicy sauces.

Pu-ehr tea is typically brewed at a lower temperature than other teas, such as green tea or black tea. This lower temperature can help preserve the tea's delicate flavors and aromas. When pairing pu-ehr tea with food, it is important to serve the tea at a temperature that will not overpower the flavors of the dish.

Here are some examples of dishes that can be enhanced by pu-ehr tea:

- Roasted meats: The rich, savory flavor of roasted meats, such as beef or lamb, can be enhanced by pu-ehr tea. The tea can be brewed at a low temperature and served alongside the meat to complement its flavors.

- Grilled vegetables: The smoky flavor of grilled vegetables, such as asparagus or bell peppers, can be enhanced by pu-ehr tea. The tea can be brewed at a low temperature and served alongside the vegetables to bring out their smoky flavor.

- Mushrooms: The earthy flavor and aroma of mushrooms, such as shiitake or portobello, can be enhanced by pu-ehr tea. The tea can be brewed at a low temperature and served alongside the mushrooms to bring out their earthy flavor and aroma.

- Curries: The spicy flavors and aromas of curries, such as chicken curry or vegetable curry, can be enhanced by pu-ehr tea. The tea can be brewed at a low temperature and served alongside the curry to bring out its spicy flavors and aromas.

Purple Tea

Pairing food and purple tea can be challenging, as the tea's unique flavor and color can sometimes clash with certain foods. However, you can create delicious and visually appealing combinations that will impress your guests and elevate your dining experience.

First, it's essential to understand the flavor profile of purple tea. Unlike green or black tea, which are typically astringent and earthy, purple tea has a sweet and fruity flavor with hints of berries and lavender. It also has a distinctive purple color that can add a visual element to your dishes.

One way to pair purple tea with food is to match its sweet and fruity flavor with sweet and fruity foods. For example, purple tea pairs well with desserts such as fruit tarts, sorbets, and crème brûlée. The tea's fruity notes can also enhance the flavor of savory dishes, such as grilled salmon with a berry sauce or chicken with a lavender honey glaze.

Another way to pair purple tea with food is to use it as an ingredient in your dishes. For example, you can infuse purple tea into a syrup or glaze and use it to coat fruits, vegetables, or meats. You can also use the tea to make a reduction sauce for your dishes or add it to marinades and dressings for added depth and complexity of flavor.

One of the most popular ways to pair purple tea with food is to use it in cocktails and mocktails. Purple tea's sweet and fruity flavors make it a perfect ingredient for refreshing summer drinks, such as a purple tea lemonade or a purple tea mojito. You can also use purple tea to make ice pops or sorbets, which can be served as a refreshing dessert or snack.

In addition to its flavor, purple tea also has a unique color that can add a visual element to your dishes. You can use the tea to make colorful syrups or glazes that can be drizzled over fruits, vegetables, or meats. You can also use it to make purple tea ice cubes, adding a pop of color to your drinks.

CHAPTER SEVEN
How to Cook with Tea

Tea is an incredibly versatile ingredient that can be used in many different ways in cooking. Its unique flavor and aroma make it a perfect addition to a wide range of dishes, from sweet desserts to savory entrees. In addition to its taste and aroma, tea has numerous health benefits that make it an excellent choice for incorporating into your cooking.

In this chapter, we will explore the reasons why using tea in cooking is a great idea and provide some tips and ideas for incorporating it into your recipes.

What Types of Teas Can You Cook With?

You might be amazed at the diversity of tea-based cooking alternatives available. From black to green to herbal, tea can add depth and flavor to a variety of dishes.

One type of tea that is commonly used in cooking is black tea. Black tea is typically strong and full-bodied, making it a great choice for dishes that require a bold flavor. It can be used to make a delicious broth for soups and stews or added to marinades for meat and vegetables.

Green tea is another popular option for cooking. This type of tea is lighter in flavor and is often used in Asian cuisine. It can be brewed, added to soups and marinades, and even used as a sauce base. Green tea is also known for its health benefits, making it a great addition to any dish.

Rooibos tea is yet another variety of tea that is frequently put to use in culinary applications. This South African tea has a slightly sweet, nutty flavor and can be used in various dishes. It can be brewed and used as a base for soups or added to marinades for a unique flavor.

Finally, herbal teas are another versatile option for cooking. From chamomile to peppermint, a wide range of herbal teas can add unique flavors to your dishes. For example, chamomile tea can be used to make a delicious tea-infused salad dressing, while peppermint tea can be added to desserts for a refreshing twist.

Infusions

Cooking with tea is a flavorful and enjoyable way to add originality to your culinary creations. Whether you're looking to add a subtle hint of tea to your meal or create a dish fully infused with tea, there are many ways to incorporate this versatile ingredient into your cooking. Tea infusions, in particular, are a quick and easy method to add tea's distinct flavors and aromas to your cuisine.

How to create a tea infusion? This involves steeping tea leaves in hot water, just as you would for a cup of tea, and then using the infused water in place of plain water in your recipe. For example, you could use an earl grey tea infusion in place of water when making a pot of rice or use a chai tea infusion as the liquid in a cake batter. The possibilities are endless, and the flavor possibilities are limited only by your imagination.

Another way to use tea in your cooking is to infuse oils or butter with tea leaves. This can be done by heating the oil or butter in a saucepan, adding the tea leaves, and allowing the mixture to steep for a few minutes. Once the tea has been infused into the oil or butter, you can strain out the leaves and use the flavored oil or butter in your cooking. For example, you could use tea-infused butter in a sautéed dish or tea-infused oil as a marinade for grilled meats or vegetables.

From savory dishes to sweet treats, here are some delicious tea infusion recipes to try at home:

Green tea and miso soup

This classic Japanese soup gets a flavor boost from the addition of green tea. To make it, simply steep a green tea bag in hot water for a few minutes, then remove the bag and add the infused water to your miso soup base. The tea will add a subtle, grassy flavor that perfectly complements the miso's umami.

Chai-spiced oatmeal

Start your day off right with a warm bowl of chai-spiced oatmeal. The spicy, fragrant flavors of the chai tea will add a delicious kick to your oatmeal. Simply steep a chai tea bag in a cup of hot water, then add the infused liquid to your oatmeal along with your choice of sweetener, milk, and toppings.

Marinades and Rubs

Tea can add a delightful and unexpected twist to your favorite recipes, whether in a marinade or rub.

Using tea in a marinade is a great way to infuse your meats, fish, or vegetables with a subtle and aromatic flavor. To make a tea marinade, start by brewing a strong cup of your favorite tea. Green tea, black tea, and oolong tea all work well in marinades, so choose whichever you prefer or have on hand.

Once your tea is brewed, let it cool to room temperature and then mix it with your other marinade ingredients. This can include soy sauce, vinegar, honey, garlic, and ginger, depending on the flavors you want to achieve. Then, pour the marinade over your chosen ingredient and let it marinate for at least an hour or overnight for the best results.

In addition to using tea in marinades, it can also be used to make flavorful rubs for meats and vegetables. To make a tea rub, combine equal parts of tea leaves and your other chosen ingredients, such as salt, pepper, herbs, and spices. Grind the mixture into a fine powder using a spice grinder or mortar and pestle, and then rub it evenly over your chosen ingredient.

For example, you could make a black tea and herb rub for grilled chicken by mixing equal parts of black tea leaves and dried herbs like rosemary and thyme. Or, you could make a green tea and spice rub for roasted vegetables by mixing equal parts green tea leaves and spices like cumin and coriander.

Broths and Poaching Liquids

One way to incorporate tea into your cooking is by using it as a base for broths and poaching liquids. Tea-infused broths add a subtle and complex flavor to soups and stews, while tea-poached eggs or fish provide a delicate and fragrant twist to your meals.

How to make a tea broth - Simply steep your favorite tea in hot water for a few minutes, then strain and use it as the base for your soup or stew. Green tea, white tea, and oolong tea are all great choices for this purpose, as they have a mild and delicate flavor that won't overpower the other ingredients. You can also add herbs and spices to the broth to enhance its flavor and add additional health benefits.

How to make a tea-poached dish – Bring a pot of tea and water to a gentle simmer, then add your ingredients and cook until they are done. Tea-poached salmon is a popular and delicious option, as the tea adds a subtle flavor and helps to keep the fish moist and tender. You can also try tea-poached eggs, which are delicious and easy to make. Simply bring the tea and water to a simmer, crack the eggs into the liquid, and cook until the whites are set and the yolks are still runny.

Cooking with tea is also a great way to reduce food waste. Instead of throwing out old tea bags or leaves, you can use them in your cooking and get the most out of your tea.

Stir-Fry

One of the most popular teas to use in cooking is genmaicha, a blend of green tea and roasted brown rice.

Genmaicha, also known as "popcorn tea," has a nutty and slightly sweet flavor that pairs well with different ingredients. It is often used in stir-fry dishes, where its bold flavor can shine.

To use genmaicha in a stir-fry, start by brewing a cup of tea and setting it aside. In a wok or large frying pan, heat up some oil over medium-high heat. Add your choice of protein and vegetables, constantly stirring until cooked to your desired doneness.

Once the protein and vegetables are cooked, pour in the brewed genmaicha and stir to incorporate it into the dish. The tea will add a rich and savory flavor to the stir-fry, complementing the other ingredients perfectly.

Smoothies

Incorporating tea into your smoothies is a simple and delicious way to add flavor and health benefits to your daily routine. Try these recipes and experiment with different teas and flavor combinations to find your perfect tea smoothie.

One recipe for a tea-infused smoothie is the <u>Green Tea Matcha Smoothie</u>. This smoothie is packed with antioxidants and has a delicious, earthy flavor. To make this smoothie, you will need the following:

- 1 cup unsweetened almond milk

- 1 scoop of green tea matcha powder

- 1 banana

- 1 cup baby spinach

- 1 tablespoon honey

Blend all ingredients together until smooth, and enjoy!

Another tasty tea smoothie recipe is the <u>Chai Tea Smoothie</u>. This smoothie has a warming, spicy flavor that is perfect for cold winter mornings. To make this smoothie, you will need the following:

- 1 cup unsweetened vanilla almond milk

- 1 chai tea bag

- 1 banana

- 1 tablespoon honey

- 1/2 teaspoon ground cinnamon

- 1/4 teaspoon ground ginger

Steep the chai tea bag in the almond milk for 5 minutes, then remove and discard the tea bag. Blend all ingredients together until smooth, and enjoy!

Baked Goods

Whether you're a seasoned baker or just starting out, incorporating tea into your recipes can result in some truly delightful treats.

One of the most popular ways to use tea in baking is by infusing it into butter or cream. This simple technique allows the tea flavor to shine through in your finished product. To infuse tea into butter or cream, heat it over low heat until it is warm. Add in your desired amount of tea leaves and let them steep for 5-10 minutes. Strain out the tea leaves and let the butter or cream cool before using it in your recipe.

One delicious recipe that utilizes this technique is <u>Earl Grey Tea Cookies</u>. To make these cookies, you will need:

- 1 cup unsalted butter infused with Earl Grey tea leaves

- 1 cup sugar

- 2 eggs

- 2 1/2 cups all-purpose flour

- 1 teaspoon baking powder

- 1/4 teaspoon salt

Preheat your oven to 375°F and line a baking sheet with parchment paper. In a large mixing bowl, beat the infused butter and sugar until the result is light and fluffy. Add in the eggs and mix until well combined. Whisk the flour, baking powder, and salt together in a separate bowl. Gradually add the dry ingredients to the wet ingredients and mix until a dough forms.

Roll the dough into small balls and place them on the prepared baking sheet. Bake the cookies for 10-12 minutes or until they are lightly golden around the edges. Allow the cookies to cool on the baking sheet for a few minutes before transferring them to a wire rack to cool completely. These cookies are perfect for dipping in your favorite cup of tea or for enjoying as a sweet treat on their own.

Another option is to use brewed tea in place of liquid ingredients in your recipes. This is a simple way to add a unique twist to your favorite baked goods recipes. For example, you could use strongly brewed black tea in place of water in a cake batter or use green tea to add flavor to cookie dough.

Last but not least, you can use tea in frosting and glazes. For a simple and tasty frosting, steep some tea leaves in milk or cream until it is strongly flavored, then strain and use the infused liquid in place of plain milk in a basic buttercream frosting recipe. You can also use brewed tea as a glaze for cakes and cookies by simply brushing it over the surface of the baked goods while they are still warm.

Seven Surprising Recipes You Can Make with Tea

<u>Sweet Tea Barbecued Chicken</u>

Sweet Tea Barbecued Chicken is a delicious twist on the traditional barbecue dish. The sweet tea adds a distinct Southern flavor to the chicken, while the barbecue sauce adds a tangy kick. This recipe will surely be a hit at your next cookout or family dinner.

To make Sweet Tea Barbecued Chicken, you will need the following ingredients:

4 pounds of chicken pieces (such as drumsticks, thighs, or breasts)

- 1 cup of sweet tea

- 1 cup of barbecue sauce

- 2 tablespoons of honey

- 1 tablespoon of apple cider vinegar

- 1 teaspoon of garlic powder

- Salt and pepper, to taste

First, preheat your grill to medium-high heat. In a small saucepan, combine the sweet tea, barbecue sauce, honey, apple cider vinegar, and garlic powder. Heat the sauce over medium heat, occasionally stirring, until it is hot and well mixed.

Next, season the chicken pieces with salt and pepper, and place them on the preheated grill. Grill the chicken for about 10 minutes per side or until it is cooked through and the internal temperature reaches 165 degrees Fahrenheit.

Once the chicken is cooked, brush it with the sweet tea barbecue sauce. Continue grilling the chicken for an additional 5 minutes or until the sauce has caramelized and the chicken is nicely glazed.

Serve the Sweet Tea Barbecued Chicken hot off the grill, with additional sauce on the side for dipping. This delicious recipe will surely be a hit at your next cookout or family dinner.

Almond-Chai Granola

Almond-Chai Granola is a nutritious breakfast option that is perfect for those looking to add a bit of flavor and spice to their morning routine. The combination of almonds, chai spices, and oats creates a unique and satisfying flavor that will awaken your taste buds and kick-start your day.

To make this tasty granola, you will need:

1 cup of rolled oats

1/2 cup of sliced almonds

- 1/4 cup of coconut oil

- 1/4 cup of honey or maple syrup

- 1 tablespoon of chai spice blend (such as cinnamon, cardamom, cloves, and ginger)

- 1/2 teaspoon of vanilla extract

Preheat your oven to 350 degrees and line a baking sheet with parchment paper. In a large mixing bowl, combine the oats and almonds and set aside. Heat the coconut oil and honey or maple syrup in a small saucepan over medium heat until melted. Remove from heat and stir in the chai spice blend and vanilla extract. Pour the mixture over the oats and almonds and stir until evenly coated.

Spread the granola mixture onto the prepared baking sheet and bake for 15-20 minutes, stirring halfway through, until golden brown and crispy. Let the granola cool completely before breaking it into pieces and storing it in an airtight container.

Enjoy your Almond-Chai Granola with milk or yogurt or as a topping for oatmeal or smoothie bowls. The chai spice blend adds a unique and warming flavor, while the almonds provide crunch and added nutrition. Try experimenting with different sweeteners and spices to create your own unique granola blend.

Black Currant Tea-Chocolate Truffles

The combination of black currant tea and chocolate is a match made in heaven. The tartness of the black currant tea balances out the sweetness of the chocolate, resulting in a truffle that is both indulgent and sophisticated.

Ingredients:

1/2 cup unsalted butter

1 cup dark chocolate chips

- 1/2 cup heavy cream

- 1/4 cup black currant tea, brewed and cooled

- 1/4 cup cocoa powder

Directions:

1. In a saucepan, melt the butter and chocolate chips over low heat. Stir constantly until smooth.

2. Add the heavy cream and black currant tea and stir until well combined.

3. Remove from heat and let the mixture cool for a few minutes.

4. Using a small cookie scoop or spoon, form the mixture into balls and place them on a parchment-lined baking sheet.

5. Roll the truffles in cocoa powder, making sure they are well coated.

6. Place the truffles in the refrigerator for at least an hour to firm up.

7. Serve the chilled truffles with a cup of hot black currant tea on the side.

Black currant tea has been gaining popularity in recent years for its health benefits, including its high levels of antioxidants and anti-inflammatory properties. By incorporating it into a decadent dessert like truffles, you can indulge in a tasty treat while reaping the tea's benefits.

In this recipe, the black currant tea is brewed and then added to the melted chocolate and butter mixture, infusing the truffles with a subtle but distinct flavor. The cocoa powder coating adds a rich, chocolatey finish to the truffles.

Chai-Spiced Tea Loaves

This chai-spiced tea loaf is a delicious and fragrant twist on traditional tea bread. Adding chai spice mix gives it a warm, spicy flavor that pairs perfectly with a cup of tea or coffee. The raisins add a touch of sweetness and the melted butter makes it moist and tender. It's a great dessert for fall and winter gatherings or a cozy treat on a cold day.

Ingredients:

- 1 cup milk

- 2 tablespoons sugar

- 1 teaspoon chai spice mix (cinnamon, cardamom, cloves, ginger, black pepper)

- 2 cups all-purpose flour

- 2 teaspoons baking powder

- 1/2 teaspoon salt

- 1/4 cup unsalted butter, melted and cooled

- 1 large egg, beaten

- 1 teaspoon vanilla extract

- 1/2 cup raisins

Directions:

1. Preheat your oven to 350°F and grease a 9x5-inch loaf pan. In a small saucepan, heat the milk over medium heat until steaming.

2. Add the sugar and chai spice mix and stir until dissolved. Remove from heat and

let cool for 10 minutes.

3. Whisk together the flour, baking powder, and salt in a large mixing bowl. In a separate bowl, whisk together the melted butter, egg, and vanilla extract.

4. Pour the wet ingredients into the dry ingredients and stir until well combined. Stir in the raisins.

5. Pour the batter into the prepared loaf pan and smooth the top with a spatula. Bake for 45-50 minutes or until a toothpick inserted into the center comes out clean.

6. Cool in the pan for 10 minutes, then transfer to a wire rack to cool completely.

Slow Cooker Green Tea Ramen

This green tea slow cooker ramen is a delicious and healthy way to enjoy ramen at home. The green tea adds a unique and refreshing flavor, while the vegetables provide a nourishing and satisfying meal. Plus, using a slow cooker makes it easy to prepare and cook without much effort.

Ingredients:

1 pack of green tea noodles

1 cup of vegetable broth

- 1 cup of water

- 1 cup of sliced mushrooms

- 1 cup of sliced bok choy

- 1 cup of sliced carrots

- 1 cup of sliced bell peppers

- 1 cup of sliced scallions

- 1 tbsp of green tea leaves

- 1 tsp of sesame oil

- 1 tbsp of soy sauce

- 1 tbsp of miso paste

Directions:

1. In a slow cooker, combine the vegetable broth, water, green tea leaves, sesame oil, and soy sauce. Stir to combine and let it come to a simmer.

2. Add the sliced mushrooms, bok choy, carrots, bell peppers, and scallions to the slow cooker. Stir to combine and let it cook for about an hour or until the vegetables are tender.

3. In the meantime, cook the green tea noodles according to the package instructions. Drain and set aside.

4. Once the vegetables are tender, add the miso paste to the slow cooker and stir to combine.

5. To serve, divide the green tea noodles into bowls and ladle the green tea slow cooker ramen over the top. Garnish with scallions, and enjoy!

Pot-Roasted Chicken with Mushrooms

The chamomile flowers not only add a subtle floral aroma to the chicken but also help keep the meat moist and tender while it roasts. The mushrooms add an earthy flavor and provide a delicious side dish to the pot-roasted chicken. This recipe is perfect for a cozy Sunday dinner or a special occasion meal.

Ingredients:

1 whole chicken

- 1 cup dried chamomile flowers

- 1 cup mixed mushrooms, sliced

- 1 onion, sliced

- 4 cloves of garlic, minced

- 1 tablespoon olive oil

- 1 tablespoon butter

- 1 teaspoon dried thyme

- Salt and pepper to taste

Directions:

1. Preheat your oven to 375 degrees F.

2. In a small bowl, mix together the dried chamomile flowers and thyme. Set aside.

3. Rub the chicken with olive oil and season it with salt and pepper.

4. Place the chicken in a roasting pan and tuck the chamomile and thyme mixture under the skin of the chicken.

5. In a separate pan, heat the butter over medium heat and add the onions, mushrooms, and garlic. Sauté until the onions are translucent and the mushrooms are softened.

6. Arrange the mushroom mixture around the chicken in the roasting pan.

7. Roast the chicken in the oven for about 1 hour or until the internal temperature reaches 165 degrees F.

8. Let the chicken rest for about 10 minutes before slicing and serving.

Green Tea Pesto Pasta

This unique and flavorful green tea pesto pasta is a delicious twist on a classic Italian dish. The green tea adds a delicate and refreshing flavor to the pesto, making it perfect for a light summer meal. Adding Parmesan cheese and garlic adds depth and richness to the dish. Plus, it's easy to make and requires only a handful of simple ingredients.

Ingredients:

1 cup fresh basil leaves

- 1/2 cup green tea leaves

- 1/2 cup grated Parmesan cheese

- 1/2 cup olive oil

- 2 cloves garlic, minced

- Salt and pepper to taste

- 1/2 pound pasta of your choice

To prepare the green tea pesto, combine the basil leaves and green tea leaves in a food processor or blender and pulse until finely chopped. Add the Parmesan cheese, olive oil, garlic, salt, and pepper and pulse until smooth.

To prepare the pasta, bring a pot of salted water to a boil and cook the pasta according to the package instructions. Drain the pasta and return it to the pot. Add the green tea pesto and toss to combine.

Serve the green tea pesto pasta hot, garnished with additional Parmesan cheese and a drizzle of olive oil, if desired.

CHAPTER EIGHT
Tea Infused Cocktails

Did you ever know that you can make cocktails using tea? Tea-infused cocktails are a unique and delicious way to enjoy your favorite beverage in a whole new way. By incorporating tea into your cocktail recipes, you can add a depth of flavor and complexity that is hard to achieve with traditional mixers.

Tea has been used in cocktails for centuries, with some of the earliest known recipes dating back to the 19th century. The versatility of tea allows it to be paired with a wide range of spirits, from gin and vodka to rum and whiskey. Whether you prefer a classic cocktail with a tea twist or a creative, modern concoction, there are countless ways to incorporate tea into your next drink.

One of the most popular ways to use tea in cocktails is to create a tea-infused syrup or simple syrup. The syrup can be used as a sweetener in cocktails, adding both flavor and complexity to the drink. This can be done by steeping your chosen tea in hot water for several minutes, then adding sugar and allowing it to dissolve. Another popular method is to use cold-brewed tea as a mixer. This involves steeping your tea in cold water for several hours or overnight, then straining the tea and using it as the base of your cocktail. Cold-brewed tea tends to have a smoother, more mellow flavor than hot-brewed tea, making it a great choice for cocktails.

There are countless teas to choose from when it comes to creating tea-infused cocktails. Black teas, such as Earl Grey and Darjeeling, are often used for their bold, robust flavors. Green teas, such as matcha and sencha, are also popular choices, as they add a refreshing, earthy flavor to cocktails. Herbal teas, such as chamomile and lavender, can also be used to add unique aromas and flavors to cocktails.

The possibilities are endless when choosing a spirit to pair with your tea-infused cocktail. Gin and vodka are both popular choices, as they have a clean, neutral flavor that allows the tea to shine. Rum and whiskey are also great options, adding depth and richness to the cocktail. Many classic cocktails can be easily adapted to include tea. The classic gin and tonic can be given a tea twist by using a tea-infused simple syrup instead of regular simple syrup. The mojito can also be transformed by using cold-brewed tea instead of traditional lime juice.

Besides these classic cocktails, countless creative and modern concoctions incorporate tea. One such example is the "Earl Grey Mar-tea-ni," which combines Earl Grey-infused gin with lemon juice and simple syrup for a refreshing, sophisticated drink. Another exciting option is the "Matcha Old Fashioned," which blends whiskey with cold-brewed matcha tea for a unique twist on the classic cocktail.

Rum Punch

Rum punch is a classic tropical cocktail that is perfect for summer sipping. The classic recipe combines rum, citrus juices, and sweetener, but this tea-infused version adds a delicious twist.

To make a tea-infused rum punch, you will need the following ingredients:

- 1 cup of brewed tea (we recommend using a fruity black tea or a spicy chai tea)

- 1 cup of dark rum

- 1/2 cup of lime juice

- 1/2 cup of orange juice

- 1/4 cup of simple syrup or honey

- 1/4 cup of grenadine

- Fresh fruit for garnish (such as orange slices, lime wedges, and berries)

To start, brew your tea and let it cool to room temperature. Next, combine all of the ingredients in a large pitcher and stir well to combine. Taste and adjust the sweetness as needed.

Pour the rum punch into glasses filled with ice and garnish with fresh fruit. You can also add a splash of sparkling water or club soda to give the drink some bubbles.

The tea-infused rum punch is a refreshing and flavorful twist on the classic cocktail. The tea adds a unique depth of flavor and pairs perfectly with citrus and rum. Plus, it's a great way to use up any leftover tea that you might have.

Sip this delicious rum punch on a hot summer day, or serve it at your next party for a tasty and unique cocktail. Cheers!

Bee's Knees

The Bee's Knees cocktail is a classic 1920s drink that has been coming back in recent years. This refreshing and flavorful cocktail is made with gin, honey, and lemon juice and is often infused with tea for an added layer of flavor and aroma.

The name "Bee's Knees" refers to the sweet and tangy combination of honey and lemon, which is said to be as smooth and delightful as a bee's knees. The use of tea in this cocktail adds depth and complexity, making it perfect for sipping on a hot summer day or as a refreshing after-dinner drink.

To make a Bee's Knees tea-infused cocktail, you will need:

- 1.5 ounces of gin

- 1 ounce of honey syrup (made by mixing equal parts honey and hot water)

- 0.5 ounces of lemon juice

- 1-2 teaspoons of your favorite tea (such as Earl Grey or jasmine)

First, steep your tea in hot water for 3-5 minutes, depending on your preferred strength. Let it cool to room temperature before mixing the cocktail.

Combine the gin, honey syrup, lemon juice, and cooled tea in a shaker. Shake well and strain into a chilled glass. Garnish with a lemon twist or a sprig of fresh mint for added flavor and aroma.

The Bee's Knees tea-infused cocktail is a delicious and sophisticated twist on a classic drink. The combination of gin, honey, lemon, and tea is refreshing and invigorating, making it the perfect choice for a summertime cocktail. So why not try making one for yourself and see why this delicious drink has been a favorite for nearly a century?

Earl Grey Martini

As a lover of tea and cocktails, I am always looking for creative ways to combine the two. One of my recent favorites is the Earl Grey Martini, which infuses the classic tea flavor into a smooth and sophisticated cocktail.

To make this delicious drink, you will need the following ingredients:

- 2 oz gin

- 1 oz Earl Grey tea syrup

- 1 oz lemon juice

- 1 oz simple syrup

- Lemon peel, for garnish

First, brew a strong cup of Earl Grey tea and let it cool completely. Once the tea is cool, mix it with equal parts of simple syrup to create a tea syrup. This will add the bold and fragrant flavor of Earl Grey to your cocktail without watering it down.

Next, combine the gin, Earl Grey tea syrup, and lemon juice in an ice-filled shaker. Shake well to combine and chill the ingredients. Strain the mixture into a chilled martini glass and garnish with a lemon peel for a citrusy aroma and a pop of color.

The result is a refreshing and sophisticated cocktail that perfectly balances the bold flavor of Earl Grey with the bright and tangy notes of lemon. It's the perfect drink to enjoy on a relaxing evening at home or to impress your guests at your next dinner party.

If you want to take this recipe to the next level, try infusing your gin with Earl Grey tea before mixing your cocktail. Simply steep a few Earl Grey tea bags in your gin for about an hour, then strain out the tea and use the infused gin in your martini. This will add an even deeper and more complex flavor to your drink.

Philadelphia Fish House Punch

Philadelphia Fish House Punch is a delicious and refreshing cocktail that originated in the historic city of Philadelphia. This tea-infused cocktail is perfect for sipping on a hot summer day or enjoying a dinner party.

The origins of the Philadelphia Fish House Punch date back to the 18th century when exclusive Fish House Club members would gather to enjoy this punch. The recipe was closely guarded and was passed down through generations of members.

The key ingredient in this punch is tea. Traditionally, black tea is used, but green or oolong tea can also add a different flavor profile. The tea is brewed and then combined with a blend of citrus juices, brandy, and dark rum. The result is a refreshing and complex cocktail perfect for any occasion.

To make Philadelphia Fish House Punch, you will need the following ingredients:

- 4 cups of brewed black tea

- 1 cup of fresh lemon juice

- 1 cup of fresh lime juice

- 1 cup of simple syrup

- 1 cup of brandy

- 1 cup of dark rum

First, brew the tea and let it cool to room temperature. In a large pitcher or punch bowl, combine the brewed tea with lemon juice, lime juice, simple syrup, brandy, and dark rum. Stir well to combine.

Serve the punch over ice and garnish with fresh mint leaves or citrus slices. This punch is delicious and served on its own, but it can also be mixed with sparkling water or ginger ale for a more refreshing and bubbly drink.

Whether you are enjoying it on a hot summer day or at a dinner party, this punch is sure to impress.

Old Fashioned

The Old Fashioned is a classic cocktail that has been around for centuries. It's made with just a few simple ingredients, including whiskey, bitters, sugar, and a twist of orange peel. However, if you want to add a new twist to this classic drink, why not try infusing it with tea?

To make a tea-infused Old Fashioned, you will need the following ingredients:

- 2 ounces of whiskey (rye or bourbon will work best)

- 1/2 teaspoon of sugar

- 2 dashes of bitters (Angostura bitters are a good choice)

- 1/2 teaspoon of loose-leaf black tea (such as Earl Grey or Darjeeling)

- Orange peel, for garnish

To begin, fill a mixing glass with ice and add the whiskey, sugar, and bitters. Stir until the sugar has dissolved, then add the loose-leaf tea and stir again to mix it in. Strain the mixture into a rocks glass filled with ice, and garnish with a twist of orange peel.

The tea will add a subtle, aromatic flavor to the Old Fashioned, making it a unique and delicious twist on the classic cocktail. You can experiment with different types of tea to find the flavor you like best. For example, you could try using a smoky lapsang souchong tea or a spicy chai tea for a more exotic flavor.

Whether you're a fan of the classic Old Fashioned or you're just looking to try something new, a tea-infused version is a great way to add a unique twist to this timeless drink. Give it a try and see how you like it!

Green Tea Vodka Gimlet

The gimlet is a classic cocktail that traditionally consists of gin or vodka, lime juice, and simple syrup. However, for a refreshing twist, try infusing your gimlet with green tea for a delicious and healthy twist on the classic drink.

To prepare this cocktail, you need these ingredients:

- 1 cup brewed green tea, cooled to room temperature

- 2 ounces vodka

- 1 ounce lime juice

- 1/2 ounce simple syrup

- Lime wheel for garnish

To make a green tea vodka gimlet, start by brewing a cup of green tea and letting it cool to room temperature. Next, add two ounces of vodka, one ounce of lime juice, and half an ounce of simple syrup to a shaker filled with ice. Add in the cooled green tea and shake well to combine.

Strain the mixture into a chilled glass and garnish with a lime wheel. The green tea adds a subtle, earthy flavor to the gimlet, while the lime juice provides a tangy kick. The vodka adds a subtle boozy punch, making this a perfect drink for a warm summer evening.

Not only is this green tea gimlet delicious, but it also has several health benefits. Green tea is packed with antioxidants, which can help improve overall health and well-being. Additionally, lime juice provides a dose of vitamin C, which can help boost the immune system.

Tea and Sherry

THE TEA LOVER'S BIBLE

As the weather begins to cool down and the leaves start to change colors, many people start to crave warm, comforting drinks. While hot tea is a classic choice, why not elevate your tea experience with a delicious tea-infused cocktail?

Sherry, a fortified wine, is the perfect base for a tea-infused cocktail. Its rich, nutty flavors pair well with a wide range of teas, from black to green tea and herbal blends.

One simple yet elegant option is the Tea and Sherry Sour. Start by steeping a strong black tea, such as earl grey or lapsang souchong, in hot water for several minutes. Strain the tea and let it cool. In a shaker, combine the tea with sherry, lemon juice, simple syrup, and a few dashes of bitters. Shake well and strain into a glass filled with ice. Garnish with a lemon twist and a sprig of mint for added freshness.

For a more exotic twist, try the Green Tea and Sherry Spritz. Start by steeping a green tea, such as matcha or sencha, in hot water for several minutes. Strain the tea and let it cool. In a shaker, combine the tea with sherry, lime juice, simple syrup, and a splash of soda water. Shake well and strain into a glass filled with ice. Garnish with a lime wedge and a sprig of mint for added freshness.

Herbal tea blends also make for delicious tea-infused cocktails. The Chamomile and Sherry Fizz is a perfect example. Start by steeping a chamomile tea blend in hot water for several minutes. Strain the tea and let it cool. In a shaker, combine the tea with sherry, lemon juice, simple syrup, and a splash of soda water. Shake well and strain into a glass filled with ice. Garnish with a lemon twist and a sprig of mint for added freshness.

Not only are these tea and sherry cocktails delicious, but they are also full of antioxidants and other health benefits. So why not try one the next time you crave a warm, comforting drink?

Hot Toddy with Tea

Hot Toddy is a classic winter cocktail made with hot water, honey, lemon, and whiskey. It is a warm and comforting drink that is perfect for sipping on a cold winter night. While the traditional Hot Toddy is made with just these four ingredients, many variations include different spirits and flavorings.

One delicious variation is the tea-infused Hot Toddy. This version uses tea as the base of the cocktail, giving it a rich and nuanced flavor that is perfect for those who love tea.

To make a tea-infused Hot Toddy, you will need:

- 1 cup of hot water

- 1 tea bag of your choice (black tea, green tea, or herbal tea)

- 1 tablespoon of honey

- 1 tablespoon of lemon juice

- 1 ounce of whiskey

First, heat the water until it is steaming hot. Place the tea bag in a mug and pour the hot water over it. Let the tea steep for about 3-5 minutes, depending on the type of tea you are using.

Next, add the honey and lemon juice to the mug and stir to combine. Make sure the honey is fully dissolved in the tea.

Finally, add the whiskey to the mug and stir again. The Hot Toddy is now ready to be enjoyed.

The tea-infused Hot Toddy is a delicious and comforting cocktail perfect for a cold winter night. The addition of tea adds a depth of flavor that will warm you up and satisfy your taste buds.

Hibiscus Margarita

Hibiscus margarita is a fantastic drink that is perfect for any occasion. This tea-infused version adds an extra layer of flavor and health benefits to the classic cocktail.

To make this hibiscus margarita, you will need these ingredients:

- 1 cup hibiscus tea

- 1/2 cup silver tequila

- 1/4 cup lime juice

- 1/4 cup orange liqueur

- 1/4 cup simple syrup

- Lime slices for garnish

To make the hibiscus tea, simply steep 1 tablespoon of dried hibiscus flowers in boiling water for 5-7 minutes. Strain the tea and let it cool before using it in the cocktail.

Combine the hibiscus tea, tequila, lime juice, orange liqueur, and simple syrup in a blender. Blend until smooth and pour into glasses filled with ice. Garnish with lime slices, and enjoy!

The hibiscus tea adds a beautiful red color to the margarita and gives it a slightly tart and fruity flavor. The combination of tequila and orange liqueur balances out the tartness and adds a hint of sweetness.

Not only is this hibiscus margarita great, but hibiscus tea is also packed with health benefits. It is high in antioxidants and has been shown to lower blood pressure and cholesterol levels. It can also aid in digestion and boost the immune system.

Green Tea Highball

Green Tea Highball is a unique cocktail that combines the health benefits of green tea with the smooth and complex flavors of Japanese whisky. This tea-infused cocktail is perfect for sipping on a warm summer day or enjoying a nightcap after a long day.

Ingredients:

- 1 cup brewed green tea (sencha or matcha)

- 1 shot of Japanese whisky (Hibiki or Nikka)

- Sparkling water or club soda

- Optional: simple syrup or honey, mint or lemon for garnish, sugar and matcha powder for rimming the glass

To make a Green Tea Highball, first, brew a cup of green tea using high-quality loose-leaf tea. We recommend using Japanese-style green tea, such as sencha or matcha, for its delicate flavor and health benefits. Once the tea has cooled, mix it with a shot of your favorite Japanese whisky. We recommend using a blended whisky, such as Hibiki or Nikka, for its smooth and well-balanced flavor.

Next, fill a highball glass with ice and pour in the green tea and whisky mixture. If you prefer a sweeter cocktail, you can add a splash of simple syrup or honey to the mixture. Top off the glass with a splash of sparkling water or club soda for added bubbles and refreshment.

To garnish your Green Tea Highball, add a sprig of fresh mint or a slice of lemon for a pop of color and flavor. You can also rim the glass with a mixture of sugar and matcha powder for a fun and flavorful twist.

CHAPTER NINE
Grow Your Own Tea Garden

If you are a tea lover, you may have thought about starting your own tea garden where you can grow tea plants and make fresh tea.

Growing your tea garden can be a rewarding and fulfilling experience, not only for the delicious cups of tea you can enjoy but also for the sense of accomplishment and connection to nature that comes with growing your plants.

Essential Equipment

If you have a passion for tea and have been considering starting your tea garden, there are a few essential pieces of equipment that you will need to successfully grow and harvest your tea leaves.

First and foremost, you will need a good quality soil thermometer to help you monitor the temperature of the soil in your tea garden. Tea plants thrive in warm, humid climates, and the ideal soil temperature for tea plants is between 70-80 degrees Fahrenheit. By monitoring the soil temperature, you can ensure that your tea plants grow optimally for maximum health and productivity.

Another essential piece of equipment for a tea garden is a watering can or hose with a fine spray attachment. Tea plants require regular watering, but be careful not to overwater, as this can lead to root rot and other problems. A fine spray attachment will help to distribute water evenly and prevent damage to the delicate tea leaves.

You will also need a good quality pair of gardening shears or scissors to harvest your tea leaves. Tea plants are typically harvested by hand, and a sharp pair of shears will make the process much easier and more efficient. Look for shears with comfortable, ergonomic handles and sharp, curved blades for the best results.

As your tea plants grow and mature, you must also protect them from pests and diseases. This can be done through organic pesticides and insecticides, such as neem oil or pyrethrum. These natural substances are safe for use in a tea garden and help keep your plants healthy and productive.

Finally, once you have harvested your tea leaves, you will need a tea drying rack or tray to properly dry the leaves before storing or using them. Tea leaves must be carefully dried to maintain their flavor and quality, and a good quality drying rack or tray will help ensure that your tea leaves are dried evenly and properly.

With these tools, you can successfully grow and harvest your own tea leaves, enjoying the benefits of fresh, high-quality tea right from your backyard.

Location

Choosing the right location is crucial when you want to make your own tea garden. The right location can mean the difference between a flourishing garden full of healthy plants and a struggling one that barely produces any tea.

First and foremost, choosing a location with plenty of sunlight is crucial. Tea plants require at least six hours of sunlight per day to thrive. A south-facing location is ideal, providing the most sunlight throughout the day.

In addition to sunlight, it's also important to consider soil quality. Before planting your garden, consider conducting a soil test to determine the pH level and make any necessary adjustments. Tea plants prefer well-draining soil with a pH level between 6.0 and 7.0. The plants may struggle to grow if your soil is too alkaline or acidic.

Another essential factor to consider is the availability of water. Tea plants require consistent watering in order to grow and produce tea leaves. Choose a location near a water source, such as a hose or rainwater catchment system, to ensure that your plants have easy access to water.

It's also a good idea to choose a location that is protected from strong winds and harsh weather. Tea plants are relatively delicate and can be damaged by strong winds or heavy rainfall. Choose a place sheltered from these elements, such as the side of a building or near a fence.

Once you've chosen the right location, it's time to prepare the soil before planting your herbal tea garden. This includes removing any weeds or debris and adding compost or other organic matter to improve the soil's nutrient content.

Choosing Tea Plants

When it comes to growing tea plants, there are many different types to choose from. The type of tea plant you choose will depend on a few factors, including the climate you live in, the available space, and your personal preferences.

One of the first things to consider when choosing a tea plant is the climate in which you live. Tea plants are native to tropical and subtropical climates, so if you live in a cooler climate, you will need to choose a tea plant that can withstand cooler temperatures. Some popular tea plants that are well-suited to cooler climates include Camellia sinensis var. sinensis, Camellia sinensis var. assamica, and Camellia sinensis var. cambodiensis.

Tea plants can grow quite large, so if you don't have a lot of space, you may want to choose a smaller variety, such as Camellia sinensis var. sinensis or Camellia sinensis var. cambodiensis. These varieties are also well-suited to container gardening, so you can still grow tea plants in pots if you don't have a lot of outdoor space.

In addition to climate and space considerations, you will also want to consider the flavor and aroma of the tea you want to grow. Camellia sinensis var. sinensis is the most commonly grown tea plant, and it is known for producing high-quality teas with a delicate and complex flavors. Camellia sinensis var. assamica is another popular tea plant, and it produces teas with a bold and robust flavor. Camellia sinensis var. cambodiensis is a newer variety of tea plants, and it is known for producing teas with a sweet and floral aroma.

Buying Tea Plants

Where do you start when it comes to buying tea plants for your tea garden? There are a few different options to consider, and now we explore some of the best places to buy tea plants for your tea garden.

Online tea plant nurseries

One of the most convenient ways to buy tea plants for your tea garden is to shop online at a tea plant nursery. Several reputable online tea plant nurseries offer a wide range of tea plants, including popular varieties like Camellia sinensis, the plant used to make most types of tea.

When shopping online for tea plants, do your research and choose a reputable nursery with a good track record and positive customer reviews. Look for a nursery that offers high-quality plants with a good selection of different tea plant varieties.

Local plant nurseries

Another option is to visit your local plant nursery and see if they have any tea plants for sale. Many plant nurseries carry a variety of herbs and other specialty plants, including tea plants.

When shopping at a local plant nursery, ask the staff for help and advice on choosing the right tea plants for your garden. They will be able to guide you on the best varieties to grow in your climate, as well as any special care instructions for the plants.

Specialty tea shops

Many specialty tea shops carry various tea-related products, including tea plants. If you have a favorite tea shop in your area, ask if they have any tea plants for sale.

Specialty tea shops are a great source of tea plants because they often carry rare and unique varieties you may not find at a plant nursery or online. Additionally, the staff at specialty tea shops are typically knowledgeable about tea and can provide valuable information and advice on caring for your tea plants.

Online marketplaces

Another option for buying tea plants is to shop on online marketplaces like eBay or Amazon. These sites offer a wide range of tea plants, including both common and rare varieties.

When shopping on online marketplaces, read the seller's description and customer reviews carefully to ensure that you are getting high-quality plants from a reputable seller. It is also a good idea to ask the seller any questions you may have about the plants, such as how they were grown and what type of care they will need.

Tea plant growers and producers

If you are looking for high-quality, fresh tea plants, you may purchase directly from a tea plant grower or producer. Many tea plant growers and producers offer tea plants for sale on their websites or at their tea farms.

Buying directly from a tea plant grower or producer can be a great way to get fresh, high-quality plants that are well-suited to your climate and growing conditions. Additionally, the staff at tea plant growers and producers are typically knowledgeable about tea. They can provide you with valuable information and advice on how to care for your tea plants.

Whatever source you use to get tea plants for your tea garden, make sure it is reliable. Remember that with a little bit of effort and care, your tea garden can thrive and provide you with delicious, fresh tea for years to come.

Maintenance

Once your tea plants are in the ground or in pots, it is important to provide them with proper care and maintenance to ensure their health and productivity. Tea plants are sensitive and require specific growing conditions to thrive, so it is important to be attentive to their needs.

Sunlight

To thrive, tea plants require at least 6 hours of direct sunlight per day. If your tea garden is located in an area with less than 6 hours of direct sunlight, consider moving it to a sunnier location or providing artificial light through grow lights. If you are growing your tea plants in pots, make sure to rotate them regularly to ensure even exposure to sunlight.

Soil

Tea plants prefer well-draining soil that is rich in nutrients. The soil should be rich in organic matter and have a pH between 6 and 7.5. If the soil is too acidic or alkaline, it can affect the flavor and quality of the tea leaves. To improve the soil quality, you can add compost or well-rotted manure to the soil.

Water

Watering your tea plants is essential to growing and maintaining a healthy tea garden. Here are a few tips to keep in mind when watering your tea plants:

- Water regularly: Tea plants need a consistent water supply to thrive. Water them at least once a week, more if the weather is particularly hot or dry.

- Use the right amount of water: Overwatering can be just as harmful as underwatering. Remember to use enough water to adequately hydrate the plants, but not so much that it causes root rot.

- Water at the right time: Water your tea plants in the morning or early afternoon to give them plenty of time to absorb the moisture before the sun goes down. Avoid watering at night, as this can lead to fungal growth.

- Use mulch: Adding a layer of mulch around your tea plants can help retain moisture and reduce the need for frequent watering.

- Monitor the soil: Use your finger or a soil moisture meter to check the moisture levels in the soil. If it feels dry, it's time to water. If it feels wet, wait a few days before watering again.

Fertilizing

Fertilizing your tea plants is crucial in growing and maintaining a healthy tea garden. Here are some tips for fertilizing your tea plants:

- Use a balanced fertilizer: Tea plants need a mix of nutrients, including nitrogen, phosphorus, and potassium. Choose a fertilizer with a balanced ratio of these nutrients, such as a 10-10-10 formula.

- Follow the manufacturer's instructions: Different fertilizers have different application rates, so it's important to follow the instructions on the label for the best results.

- Fertilize during the growing season: Tea plants are most active during the warmer months, so it's best to fertilize them when they are actively growing.

- Avoid overfertilizing: It's possible to give your tea plants too much fertilizer, which can lead to excess growth and reduced quality of the tea leaves. Use a soil test to determine the nutrient levels in your soil and adjust your fertilization accordingly.

- Consider using organic fertilizers: Tea plants are sensitive to chemical fertilizers, so it may be best to use organic options such as compost or bone meal.

Pruning

Pruning your tea plants can help to encourage healthy growth and improve the quality of the tea leaves that are produced. Here are some tips for pruning your tea plants:

- Prune the plants in early spring before new growth begins.

- Remove any dead or diseased branches, as well as any branches that are growing inward or crossing over other branches.

- Cut back the shoots that have grown too long or have become leggy.

- Trim the shoots to an outward-facing bud to encourage new growth to grow outward and increase the plant's density.

- Avoid pruning more than one-third of the plant's canopy at a time, as this can stress the plant.

- Use clean, sharp pruning tools to make precise cuts.

Pests and diseases

One of the main challenges faced by tea growers is dealing with insect pests and diseases that can attack and damage plants.

Some common insect pests affecting tea plants include tea leafhoppers, tea thrips, and tea mites. These insects can cause damage to the leaves, stems, and buds of the plant, which can lead to reduced growth and yield. Tea plants are also vulnerable to various diseases, including tea mosaic virus, tea blight, and tea yellow mottle virus. These diseases can cause symptoms such as yellowing or necrosis of the leaves, stunted growth, and reduced yield.

To prevent and control these insect and disease challenges, tea growers can use a combination of cultural practices, such as proper pruning, fertilization, and irrigation, as well as chemical control measures, such as insecticides and fungicides.

As a tea grower, you must regularly monitor your plants for signs of insect or disease problems and take action as soon as possible to prevent further spread and damage. By proactively addressing these challenges, you can ensure that your plants are healthy and productive.

Harvesting and Processing

First, it's important to know that not all tea plants are ready to be harvested at the same time. The optimal time to harvest will depend on the variety of tea plants and the desired tea type. For example, white and green teas are typically harvested earlier in the season when the leaves are young and tender. At the same time, black and oolong teas generally are harvested later in the season when the leaves are more mature.

To determine when your tea plants are ready to be harvested, take a close look at the leaves. They should be a vibrant green color and have a smooth, glossy appearance. The leaves should also be relatively large and plump, which indicates that they are full of flavorful oils and nutrients.

When you're ready to harvest, carefully pluck the leaves from the stems using your fingers or a pair of scissors. Be sure to avoid pulling or tearing the leaves, as this can damage the delicate tea plant and affect the quality of the tea.

Once you've harvested your tea leaves, the next step is to wither them. This process involves exposing the leaves to cool, dry air to remove excess moisture and soften the leaves. This can be done by laying the leaves on a clean, dry surface or hanging them in a well-ventilated area.

After the leaves have withered, the next step is to roll them. To roll the leaves, gently press and twist them between your palms or use a rolling tool, such as a rolling pin or wooden dowel. This process helps break down the leaves' cell walls and release the flavorful oils and aromas.

Once the leaves have been rolled, they need to be dried to preserve their flavor and prevent them from going bad. This can be done by laying the leaves on a clean, dry surface or using a drying machine. The leaves should be dried until they are brittle and crumbly to the touch. After this phase, they are ready to be packaged and stored. Be sure to store the tea in an airtight container in a cool, dry place to maintain its freshness and flavor.

Other Plants You Can Grow

Growing a variety of plants in your tea garden can bring numerous benefits and add diversity to your tea blends. Here are a few reasons why you should consider growing other plants in your tea garden:

- Flavor diversity: Growing a variety of plants in your tea garden allows you to experiment with different flavors and create unique and diverse tea blends. For example, you can mix peppermint and lemon balm for a refreshing and uplifting blend, or chamomile and lavender for a calming and relaxing blend.

- Health benefits: Different plants have different health benefits, and growing a variety of plants in your tea garden allows you to choose plants that cater to your specific health needs. For example, peppermint can aid in digestion, while chamomile can help with sleep and relaxation.

- Aesthetic value: A tea garden that consists of a variety of plants adds visual interest and beauty to your garden. Different plants have different colors, textures, and shapes, and combining them can create a stunning and visually appealing garden.

In the following pages, we will discuss the various plants you can consider growing in your tea garden, beyond the traditional camellia sinensis plant used for making traditional tea. From herbs to flowers, there are numerous options to choose from and experiment with to create unique and diverse tea blends.

Peppermint

Peppermint (Mentha piperita) is a perennial herb that is often used in herbal teas for its refreshing and invigorating aroma. It is a popular choice for tea gardens due to its easy care and versatility in tea blends. Here are some features, benefits, and tips for growing peppermint in your tea garden:

Features: Peppermint is a herb that grows up to 2 feet tall and has dark green, crinkled leaves and small, pink or white flowers. It has a strong, minty aroma and taste, which makes it a popular choice for tea blends.

Benefits: Peppermint has numerous health benefits, including aiding in digestion, relieving nausea and headaches, and boosting the immune system. It also has a refreshing and invigorating aroma, which can help to energize and invigorate the senses.

Tips for growing: Peppermint is a hardy plant that is easy to grow in most climates. It prefers well-draining soil and full sun to partial shade. It is a fast-growing plant and can spread quickly, so it is best to plant it in containers or in an area where it can be contained. To harvest peppermint for use in tea, simply snip off a few leaves and stems when needed. Peppermint can also be dried and stored for later use.

Sage

Sage (Salvia officinalis) is a popular herb that has been used for centuries for its medicinal and culinary properties. It is a perennial herb with gray-green leaves and a refreshing and invigorating aroma. Sage is often used in herbal teas for its calming and soothing effects, as well as its ability to aid in digestion. If you're looking to add a new plant to your tea garden, consider growing sage.

Features: Sage is a hardy herb that can tolerate a variety of growing conditions. It has gray-green leaves and produces small, purplish-blue flowers in the summer. Sage is a perennial plant, meaning it will come back year after year if properly cared for. It grows to a height of about 2-3 feet and has a spread of about 1-2 feet.

Benefits: Sage has a number of health benefits when consumed in tea form. It has been shown to help with digestion, reduce inflammation, and improve memory and cognitive function. Sage is also often used to help with sleep and relaxation and has even been used to treat colds and flu.

Tips for Growing:

1. Choose a location in your garden that gets plenty of sunlight, as sage needs at least six hours of sunlight per day to thrive.

2. Prepare the soil by adding compost or well-rotted manure to improve drainage and nutrient content. Sage grows best in well-draining soil with a pH between 6.0 and 7.0.

3. Plant sage seeds or seedlings in the spring, spacing them about 18 inches apart. Water the plants well after planting and continue to water regularly, especially during dry periods.

4. Fertilize the plants once a month with a balanced fertilizer to encourage growth.

5. Prune the plants regularly to keep them looking neat and encourage new growth.

Lemon Balm

Lemon balm (Melissa officinalis) is a perennial herb that is native to the Mediterranean region. It is a member of the mint family and has a refreshing and uplifting citrusy aroma that is often used in herbal teas for its calming effects. Lemon balm is a hardy plant that is easy to grow and maintain, making it an excellent choice for your tea garden.

Features: Lemon balm has delicate, green leaves that are oval-shaped and have a crinkled texture. The leaves are fragrant and have a lemony aroma when crushed. Lemon balm plants have small white or pale yellow flowers that bloom in the summer and attract bees and other pollinators. The plants can grow up to two or three feet in height and width, and they prefer well-draining soil and full sun to partial shade.

Benefits: Lemon balm has numerous health benefits and is often used in herbal teas for its calming and relaxing effects. It has been shown to reduce anxiety, improve sleep, and boost cognitive function. Lemon balm is also rich in antioxidants and has been shown to have antiviral properties, making it useful in treating cold sores and other viral infections. In addition to its health benefits, lemon balm adds a refreshing and uplifting flavor to tea blends, making it an excellent choice for those looking to add some variety to their tea garden.

Here are a few tips for growing lemon balm in your tea garden:

1. Choose a sunny spot in your garden with well-draining soil. Lemon balm prefers full sun to partial shade, and well-draining soil helps prevent the plants from becoming waterlogged.

2. Plant lemon balm in the spring, after the last frost has passed. You can either start lemon balm from seeds or purchase plants from a nursery.

3. Water lemon balm regularly, but avoid overwatering. The plants prefer evenly moist soil, but too much water can cause the roots to rot.

4. Prune lemon balm regularly to encourage new growth and prevent the plants

from becoming overgrown.

5. Harvest lemon balm in the summer, when the plants are in full bloom. Cut the stems just above a leaf node and dry the leaves in a cool, dry place. Once the leaves are dry, store them in an airtight container until ready to use.

Lemon Verbena

Lemon verbena, also known as Aloysia citrodora, is a perennial shrub native to South America. It is widely known for its lemony aroma and is often used in herbal teas for its refreshing and uplifting qualities. If you're looking to add some diversity to your tea garden, lemon verbena is a great plant to consider.

Features: Lemon verbena is a fast-growing shrub that can reach up to 4-5 feet in height. It has green, narrow, and pointed leaves that give off a strong lemon scent when crushed. The plant produces small, white, and star-shaped flowers in the summer. Lemon verbena is hardy in USDA zones 8-11 and can be grown as a perennial in these regions. It can also be grown as an annual in cooler climates.

Benefits: Lemon verbena is rich in antioxidants and has several health benefits. It has a refreshing and uplifting aroma that can help boost your mood and reduce stress. It is also believed to have antibacterial and anti-inflammatory properties, making it a great addition to your tea blends for aiding digestion and reducing inflammation.

Tips for growing:

1. Plant lemon verbena in well-draining soil in a location that receives full sun.

2. Water the plant regularly, making sure not to overwater as it can cause root rot.

3. Fertilize the plant once a month with a balanced fertilizer.

4. Prune the plant regularly to encourage new growth and prevent it from becoming leggy.

5. Harvest the leaves just before the plant flowers, as this is when the leaves contain

the highest concentration of essential oils.

Chamomile

Chamomile (Matricaria recutita) is an annual herb with small white flowers and a sweet, apple-like aroma. It is native to Europe, North Africa, and Asia, but is now cultivated worldwide. Chamomile is a popular ingredient in herbal teas and is known for its calming and relaxing properties. It is also used in aromatherapy, skincare, and as a natural remedy for various ailments.

Features: Chamomile plants have delicate, fern-like leaves and small white flowers with yellow centers. The flowers are harvested when they are fully open, typically during the summer months. Chamomile plants grow to a height of about 12-24 inches and have a spreading habit. They prefer well-draining soil and full sun to partial shade.

Benefits: Chamomile has numerous health benefits and has been used for centuries for its calming and relaxing properties. It is often used as a natural remedy for insomnia, anxiety, and stress. It is also believed to have anti-inflammatory and digestive properties and is often used to soothe digestive issues and skin irritations. Chamomile tea has a soothing and relaxing effect on the body and is often consumed before bedtime to promote sleep.

Tips for growing: Chamomile is relatively easy to grow and can be grown from seeds or purchased as seedlings. Here are a few tips for growing chamomile in your tea garden:

1. Choose a sunny spot with well-draining soil for your chamomile plants.

2. Sow the seeds directly in the ground or in pots in the spring, after the threat of frost has passed.

3. Keep the soil moist, but not waterlogged. Chamomile plants prefer well-draining soil.

4. Fertilize the plants with a balanced fertilizer once a month.

5. Pinch off the flowers when they are fully open and dry them in a cool, dark place for use in your tea blends.

Lavender

Lavender is a beautiful and fragrant herb that has been used for centuries in various applications, including as a natural remedy and in perfumes and cosmetics. It is also a popular choice for growing in a tea garden due to its soothing and calming properties, as well as its delicate and refreshing aroma.

Features: Lavender (Lavandula angustifolia) is a perennial herb that belongs to the mint family and is native to the Mediterranean region. It has a woody stem and long, narrow leaves that are gray-green in color. The plant is known for its fragrant purple flowers, which bloom from late spring to early summer. Lavender has a sweet and floral aroma that is often used in herbal teas for its calming and relaxing effects.

Benefits: Lavender has numerous health benefits, making it a great addition to your tea garden. It has a calming effect on the body and mind, making it helpful for reducing stress and anxiety. It can also aid in sleep and relaxation, making it a great choice for a bedtime tea. Lavender has antibacterial and antiviral properties, making it helpful for boosting the immune system and promoting overall health and wellness.

Tips for growing: Lavender is relatively easy to grow and thrives in well-draining soil in full sun. It is a drought-tolerant plant and does not require frequent watering. However, it is vital to water the plant deeply and consistently, especially during dry spells. Lavender can be prone to pests and diseases, so keep an eye out for any signs of infestation or illness and take the necessary steps to address them. To harvest lavender for use in your tea blends, it is best to pick the flowers when they are in full bloom and dry them in a well-ventilated place. Once dried, the flowers can be stored in an airtight container for future use.

Rose

Roses are beautiful flower that adds a touch of elegance and sophistication to any garden. While often thought of as simply ornamental plants, roses can also be used in tea blends to add a sweet and floral aroma. Growing roses in your tea garden can add diversity to your tea blends and bring numerous health benefits.

Features: Roses are perennial shrubs that are native to Asia, Europe, and North America. They come in a variety of colors, including red, pink, yellow, and white, and have fragrant flowers that bloom in the summer. The petals of the rose can be dried and used in tea blends, while the hips (the fruit of the rose plant) can also be used in tea blends and are high in vitamin C.

Benefits: Roses are high in antioxidants, which can help to protect against free radicals and reduce inflammation. Roses are also known to have calming and soothing effects, making them a great addition to tea blends for relaxation and stress relief.

Tips for Growing:

1. Choose a sunny location with well-draining soil. Roses need plenty of sunlight and well-draining soil to thrive.

2. Water regularly, but avoid overwatering. Roses need regular watering, but be sure not to overwater, as this can lead to root rot.

3. Fertilize regularly. Use a balanced fertilizer, such as a 10-10-10 formula, to ensure that your roses receive all the nutrients they need.

4. Prune regularly. Prune your roses regularly to remove dead or diseased branches and encourage new growth.

5. Protect from pests and diseases. Keep an eye out for pests and diseases, such as aphids and black spot, and take appropriate measures to control them.

Growing your own tea garden may take time and effort, but the result of delicious, homegrown tea is well worth it. Not only will you be able to enjoy the unique flavors and aromas of your tea, but you will also have the satisfaction of knowing that you grew it yourself. So why not give it a try and start your own tea garden today?

Conclusion

Thank you, dear reader, for joining me on this journey through the world of tea. I hope you have enjoyed learning about this fascinating beverage and that it has enriched your life somehow.

From its origins in ancient China to its widespread popularity, tea has been a cultural touchstone, a source of comfort and enjoyment, and a symbol of hospitality and conviviality.

Today, tea is enjoyed worldwide, with over 3 billion cups consumed daily. In many cultures, tea is more than just a drink - it's a way of life. In Japan, for example, the tea ceremony is an essential part of the culture, with elaborate rituals and precise movements used to prepare and serve the tea. In the Middle East, tea symbolizes hospitality, with hosts often serving tea to guests as a sign of welcome and friendship.

But beyond its cultural significance, tea is also a source of comfort and enjoyment. For many people, a cup of tea is a ritual that helps to calm the mind and relax the body. The warm, soothing liquid can be a welcome respite from the stresses of daily life, and the act of preparing and sipping tea can be a form of meditation or self-care.

Reading this guide taught you that tea has numerous health benefits, from reducing stress and aiding in weight loss to improving mental clarity and digestion. But one of the main reasons for the enduring popularity of tea is the vast range of available flavors and aromas. Whether you prefer delicate green teas, robust black teas, or refreshing herbal blends, there is a tea out there to suit every taste and mood.

In short, tea is more than just a beverage - it's a way of life and a source of comfort and enjoyment for millions of people. Whether you're a seasoned tea lover or a newcomer to the world of tea, I hope this book has given you a glimpse into the fascinating world of tea culture and inspired you to explore the many wonderful flavors and aromas that tea has to offer. As you continue on your journey of discovering different types of tea, I encourage you to keep experimenting with different blends and flavors. From the bold and earthy flavors of black tea to the delicate and floral notes of white tea, the world of tea is full of endless possibilities.

I am grateful for your support and look forward to sharing more tea-related knowledge with you in the future.

Until then, cheers to a cup of your favorite tea!

Thanks

F irst of all, thank you for purchasing *The Tea Lover's Bible*. I know you could have picked any number of books to read, but you picked this book, and for that, I am incredibly grateful. I hope that it added value and quality to your everyday life.

If you enjoyed this book and found some benefit in reading this, I'd like to hear from you and hope that you could take some time to post a review on Amazon. Your feedback and support will help me to improve his writing craft significantly for future projects and make this book even better. I wish you the best in all that you do!

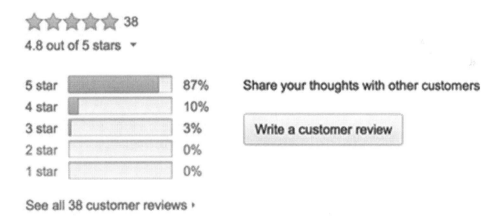

About the Author

Lydia Merrill is a certified Dietician and Nutritionist with over 20 years of experience counseling individuals on sustainable weight management and disease prevention.

She is the best-selling author of several cookbooks and is passionate about tea. In her years of practice, Merrill has helped countless individuals improve their health and well-being through dietary and lifestyle changes. She is known for her approachable and practical advice and her ability to make healthy eating enjoyable and sustainable.

When she's not working, Merrill can be found experimenting in the kitchen or sipping on her favorite cup of tea.

www.bonusliber.com

"There are few hours in life more agreeable than the hour dedicated to the ceremony known as afternoon tea"

– Henry James

Made in the USA
Las Vegas, NV
20 January 2024

84631941R00083